KT-102-786

Soup, Beautiful Soup

Previous books by Felipe Rojas-Lombardi

The Art of South American Cooking

The A to Z No-Cook Cookbook

Felipe Rojas-Lombardi Teaches George Plimpton His Game
Cookery Recipes (*with Jean Dalrymple*)

Soup, Beautiful Soup

Felipe Rojas-Lombardi

An Owl Book
Henry Holt and Company
New York

Copyright © 1985, 1992 by Felipe Rojas-Lombardi
All rights reserved, including the right to reproduce
this book or portions thereof in any form.
Published by Henry Holt and Company, Inc.,
115 West 18th Street, New York, New York 10011.
Published in Canada by Fitzhenry & Whiteside Limited,
91 Granton Drive, Richmond Hill, Ontario L4B 2N5.

Library of Congress Cataloging-in-Publication Data

Rojas-Lombardi, Felipe.
Soup, beautiful soup / Felipe Rojas-Lombardi.
p.   cm.
"An Owl book."
Includes index.
1. Soups.   I. Title.
TX757.R725   1992
641.8'13—dc20   91-31068
                                            CIP

ISBN 0-8050-1939-1

Henry Holt books are available at special discounts
for bulk purchases for sales promotions, premiums,
fund-raising, or educational use. Special editions
or book excerpts can also be created to specification.

For details contact:
Special Sales Director
Henry Holt and Company, Inc.
115 West 18th Street
New York, New York 10011

First published in hardcover in
1985 by Random House, Inc.
Revised Owl Edition—1992

Printed in the United States of America
Recognizing the importance of preserving
the written word, Henry Holt and Company, Inc.,
by policy, prints all of its first editions
on acid-free paper. ∞

1   3   5   7   9   10   8   6   4   2

TO THE MEMORY OF JAMES BEARD

Acknowledgments

My special thanks to Irene Sax for her invaluable help in editing and shaping the original manuscript. And thanks also to my assistant, Rosemarie Aldin, for her work on the new recipes, and to my friend Jack Ceglic.

Contents

Foreword to
the Original Edition
by Craig Claiborne

For a good many years I've been pleased to "borrow" the observations of M. F. K. Fisher, to my mind the finest and most knowledgeable person who writes about food. Years ago she noted that the basis of French cooking is butter, that of Italy olive oil, of Germany lard and of Russia sour cream. Water or drippings are attributed to the English kitchen, and to those of America the flavor of innumerable tin cans.

I am persuaded it is because of this that Americans, by and large, have never spent a great deal of time making soups in the home. From the cradle they are taught to sip on something that came out of a tin. If you look at the roster of traditional American soups in almost any reputable volume, the list is very small. There is, of course, clam chowder and Charleston she-crab, black bean, chicken, Philadelphia pepper pot and snapper soups, but other than these there isn't a great deal to brag about.

To my mind and appetite this is a lamentable state of affairs, for I consider soups potentially one of the great attributes of a meal—and at times one of the greatest dishes on which to feed as a meal in itself. Felipe Rojas-Lombardi is without question one of the most creative chefs in this country. His range and imagination are vast, and the soups in this volume represent some of his finest work. He is a genius with inspiration, and all the soups listed here are endowed with exceptional creativity.

This book should go far in broadening this nation's interest in the art of soup-making. It should also go far in improving the American table!

Introduction

If you can boil water, you can make soup. In fact, all that our caveman ancestors had to know before they cooked soup was how to make a fire. They made soup even before they invented cooking pots. They would heat stones in the fire and put the red-hot stones in a hollowed-out tree trunk filled with water. The water would boil; they'd add roots, meat or anything edible that was around; and there it was. Soup!

This book is about one of the oldest and most basic cooking techniques in history. But it's also about an attitude to cooking, one that may be new to you. It's about having fun in the kitchen, experimenting and taking chances.

Because that's what I've done, and that's how this book was written.

Making soup is one of the most creative ways to cook. While there are, of course, great classic soup recipes, you won't find them in these pages. Rather, you will find the end result of the fun and excitement I had in my kitchen as I worked on these wonderful soups, and the experiences and memories of a lifetime spent working with food. I love soups, whether they are hot or chilled, whether they are made with stock, milk or just plain tap water.

My mother grew up in a traditional Italian home where the kitchen was the most important place in the house. She was a wonderful cook. Father was a Chilian of Spanish and German descent, and I was born in Peru, the land of potatoes, corn and peppers. When I was growing up, there was soup at the start of every lunch and dinner. It was usually a *chupe,* or chowder, a creamy broth with corn, potatoes, squash, fish and chiles. When I was ill, the soup I remember was a thin lamb broth my grandmother made. She would mash a piece of lean lamb neck on the *batán,* a large stone which is the equivalent of a mortar and pestle, put it in a bowl and pour boiling water over it. It was a little bland, but an effective medicine.

At a young age, I left home to experience other cultures and new cuisines. I cooked in France, Italy and Spain. Up in the Basque country I learned everything there is to know about raising, processing and cooking lamb right from the shepherds.

When I arrived in New York, I was most fortunate to meet James Beard, and subsequently became his assistant. For five years I helped him with his cooking school, traveling with him extensively throughout America and Europe and working on a variety of interesting projects. It was Jim who made me realize the seriousness and scope of my profession, and its great excitement and joy. He also taught me to look at the whole range of the foods of the world with an unprovincial eye. Jim loved to mix foods, to experiment with flavors and textures, to combine ingredients and techniques from every country in the world. And Jim loved soup because he felt it was the food that allowed the cook the most freedom to be creative.

Thus, as you leaf through the pages of this book you will see *chupes, mariscadas* and *aguaditos* from South America, bisques and stocks from France, a borscht from Rumania, a *marmitako* from Spain and a *porchero* from the Philippines. All grew out of my life and cooking heritage.

I love to mix foods from all over as long as they fit the logic of the dish and of the palate, and soup provides the greatest outlet for my passion of combining different foods. Fortunately, we are able to get foods from all over the globe today, and so our horizons are nearly limitless. Food has always been international, with products that originated in one area spreading throughout the world. We think of the potato as native to Iowa, or at least Ireland; but it came from my native Peru, where there are still an immense number of varieties. Corn, which originated at the foot of the Andes and was spread over the entire continent by birds, found its way to Europe through returning colonists. Okra, which we think of as native to our American South, is from Africa. And tomatoes, which dominate Southern Italian cooking, were unknown in Europe until a few hundred years ago. So bringing together different food cultures and mixing all sorts of seemingly diverse ingredients in a single recipe is really the most logical thing to do.

Personal taste plays a part in the creation of any recipe, and in my cooking I have a tendency to use certain flavors over and over again, alone, in pairs or all together. They are pepper, ginger and garlic, a trio I find unbeatable.

PEPPERS

In Peru we use an enormous variety of peppers to add taste, texture, color and heat to our food, and it is unquestionably my South American origin that makes me adore peppers (which you know by the Mexican name *chile,* but which we in Peru call *ají*). I think they can go into nearly everything. I even put chiles into chocolate sauce and the sugary syrups I use for poaching fruits! It is known that chiles have a lot of vitamin A and much more vitamin C than oranges.

There are hundreds of kinds of peppers, and unfortunately, their names change from one place to another. But now, in most markets, you should be able to find large green *chiles poblanos,* medium-size *jalapeños* and tiny *serranos.* Use them interchangeably, remembering the rule of thumb that the larger the pepper is, the sweeter and milder it is; the smaller, the hotter.

When you buy fresh chiles, wrap them in paper towels and store them in a cool room or the vegetable bin of your refrigerator. Don't put them in plastic bags, as they will rot. I often buy a big bunch of fresh peppers and sew them together with a needle and thread to form a loose garland, then hang them in a cool, dry spot.

You have to take care in using peppers, whether fresh, dried or canned. All the flavor is in the pulp; the seeds are indigestible and carry no taste, only irritating oils. When you use peppers, first cut them open, then scrape out and discard the seeds—and wash your hands carefully. I've seen too many people forget to do this and then rub their eyes, with painful results.

Commercially dried chiles are sold in Oriental and Hispanic markets and are just as good as the ones you dry at home. Remove the seeds as you would from fresh peppers, and wash your hands. What of the red pepper flakes that come in shake-top jars? I've often found myself in kitchens when I've needed something to give heat and found nothing but a jar of red pepper flakes. I would spill out the contents and then try to separate the bits of pulp from the seeds. I tell you, there are a lot more seeds than pulp in those jars! If you have nothing else, tie the red pepper flakes in cheesecloth and use the bag as you would a bouquet garni.

If you can't find fresh or dried hot peppers, you can certainly find canned green jalapeños packed in water or brine. Just drain them and use them. I think you'll find them plenty hot.

Chiles, however, are unpredictable, their heat varying with the conditions in which they grow. You'll have to taste as you learn to use them. I find them a marvelous way to season food because they are vegetables and not as hard on the stomach as spices. Black pepper, which is a spice, can affect the stomach. Chiles can be too hot for the tongue, but never for the stomach.

GINGER

To understand ginger you must realize that it, too, is a vegetable and has the same bite as other root vegetables, such as turnips and radishes. But with the ginger comes a refreshingly sweet and lemony perfume. I wouldn't know how to survive without ginger!

Sometimes in the spring I can buy tender purple shoots of young ginger, which I serve raw with meat or fish, as though it were a pickle; for instance, you eat a piece of duck and then a bite of young ginger. This is a good thing too with meaty soups, such as pot-au-feu or *sancochado*. If you don't have delicate young ginger, you can pickle mature ginger by slicing the root very thin and then marinating it in your favorite vinegar; raspberry vinegar makes an especially fragrant pickle.

But most of the time I buy the sculptured knobs of ginger at the vegetable counter and store them in a cool spot near the potatoes. If I'm making stock or stew, I just break off an inch of the root, slit it, and toss it into the pot. For other dishes I usually pare it and then either julienne it with the grain of the vegetable or chop it with a knife or in the food processor. In this book there's a recipe for chicken soup that uses a great deal of julienned ginger as a vegetable, and I think it's fantastic.

Powdered ginger is fine for baking, but it can't really be used in other cooking. It has no freshness, no glamour. If you want real excitement, the next time your cake recipe calls for powdered ginger, add grated fresh ginger to the batter instead. The whole cake will come alive!

GARLIC

The third of my trio of vegetables is the most familiar of all. It's hard to believe that not so long ago North American cooks were suspicious of garlic as a foreign, low-class, and probably unhealthy food. Now we find garlic in every market—not just the familiar plump bulbs, but tiny purple Greek garlic and huge elephant garlic. When you choose among them, remember that the larger the garlic clove is, the milder and sweeter its taste will be. So if a recipe calls for a clove of garlic, you'll get more or less the same result no matter what size you use. Just be sure the garlic is fresh, plump and juicy. (Dry garlic cloves give a bitter taste to everything they touch.)

What does matter, however, is the way the garlic is processed. Chopping and cooking methods change the taste dramatically. At one extreme is raw chopped garlic: strong, sharp and pungent. At the other extreme is garlic that is roasted for an hour until it is soft and sweet, and can be used as sauce for roasted meat or spread on bread like butter. As a matter of fact, that's what happens with some of the whole cloves of garlic that simmer for an hour or more in our soups: they develop the sweetness of a cooked vegetable.

When you add garlic to soup, its form determines how strong the taste will be. You may want to rub the inside of the tureen with a clove of garlic for the faintest fragrance. Whole cloves, or bulbs cut in half, give a strong yet gentle aroma when they are simmered in soup. Crushed cloves emit a more pungent taste. And many recipes start by asking you to sauté minced garlic in oil: a good way to control its flavor as long as you don't burn the garlic. If you do, throw it out and start over again, because you'll never get rid of the acrid taste.

A garlic press is a useless implement. By the time you clean it, you might as well have minced the garlic properly by hand. And powdered garlic and garlic salt are, of course, hopeless. Just forget about them.

STOCKS

When young cooks start working, the first thing they learn to make are stocks, deeply flavored broths made by cooking bones and aromatic vegetables together in liquid for a long time. With a good stock on hand you'll never have to be without soup. And you'll have the satisfaction of making something wonderful with ingredients that might otherwise have been thrown out.

Although stock takes a long time to cook, the actual work is as short as tossing bones and vegetables into a potful of water and turning on the stove. You don't even have to pare the vegetables, since you'll be discarding them once all their goodness has been extracted.

Whenever you have a chicken carcass, beef bones or shrimp shells left over, put them in plastic bags in the freezer. Then, when you have a day at home, get out the bones or shells and make stock. Go through the vegetable bin and take out the celery and carrots that are beginning to get limp. You don't have to use prime ingredients for stock. Celery tops give as good results as the greenest outer stalks of celery, and bones from roasted birds provide a richer broth than breast of chicken. Once your stock is made, cool it, skim the fat from the top and freeze it in small, well-marked containers. There will be liquid gold in your freezer.

Some of the recipes in this book seem not to use stock. If you look at them closely, you'll see that some of them have a step where you are asked to parboil some bones or vegetables in water; with that step, you are creating a quick stock. But be assured, many of these recipes need only water.

Canned stocks are fine but tend to be salty. When you use canned chicken or beef broth, dilute each can with one can of water, and add more salt only when the soup is cooked. If all you have are bouillon cubes, however, I'd advise you to throw them away and use plain tap water instead. The cubes have an artificial flavor and chemical undertaste that never seem to disappear and tend to cover the freshness of the other ingredients.

BREAD

I can't think of soup without thinking of bread. Crusty white baguettes complement all soups, of course, as they do nearly all other foods. But be as free in your choice of bread as you are in the choice of ingredients for your soups, heeding only your feel for what goes with what. I love sour rye bread with vegetable soups, especially when the soup contains fennel. Corn bread goes with chowders, and nutty quick breads with fruit soups, sourdough with fish soups, chewy pita with thick stewlike soups, crisp crackers with delicate broths (like biscuits with tea). And right on target is dense black bread with cabbagy borscht. If you have soup and bread, you need nothing more to make a meal.

EQUIPMENT

All you need to make soup is a pot or pan in which to boil water.

I love *sautoirs,* wide pans with high straight sides that look like skillets. They're something between a saucepan and a skillet. A *sautoir* is wonderful when you're making a soup with big chunks of meat, cabbage or mussels to move about, because it lets you get at them easily with your tongs. Of course, the wide surface promotes evaporation, and you'll have to keep the cover on when you're not adding or taking out ingredients.

Another useful pot is a stockpot, a tall straight-sided saucepan with handles on both sides. These are especially good for making stocks because as the heat rises and falls in the liquid all the ingredients blend wonderfully. The small surface area means that the liquid doesn't boil away before it has time to extract all the goodness from the vegetables and bones.

As for material, copper, of course, is fabulous and conducts heat beautifully. But stainless steel is more practical, since it doesn't have to be retinned as copper does. And the fact that stainless is not such a good conductor of heat doesn't matter when you're making stock or a thin soup, since the liquid in the pot will help do the job. Aluminum conducts heat wonderfully, nearly as well as copper, and makes beautiful *sautoirs*. But you have to be careful when you use aluminum, which has a tendency to interact with acid foods like tomatoes and spinach. Even milk and cream will change color and become metallic when they're cooked in aluminum; I've had cheese soups turn gray in aluminum pots. Enamel, ceramic or glass are best for cream or cheese soups. Iron is a wonderful cooking material, although it requires maintenance. You have to keep it oiled to prevent rust, and you can't let food stand in iron for any time. Enameled steel is very good and can often be brought to the table for service, but it is very heavy when you're using a large volume of liquid. But don't worry about your pots. Use whatever you have.

You'll also want a colander, ladles and tongs, strainers and cheesecloth. I use a food mill regularly, and it's good to have a blender and a food processor as well. (A blender is more efficient for thin soups because the liquid will not seep out the bottom as it will in a food processor.) Once you get involved with making soups, you'll find that you use every bit of equipment in your kitchen. For just as soup-making calls on all the skills you have—dicing and sautéing, stir-frying and skimming—so does it make use of all the pots, pans, knives and cleavers, all the whisks and wooden spoons, you have.

But the most important piece of equipment you can bring to soup-making is your imagination and your spirit of fun. Enjoy these recipes, and go on to invent your own.

All the recipes in this book serve six to eight.

MORE BEAUTIFUL SOUPS

Following the publication of the first edition of this book in 1985, I received many requests for my onion soup as well as for some fruit soups. I promised that I would respond to these requests in the second edition of the book and also add some other unique soups. So here they are, twenty more beautiful soups, starting on page 157.

Vegetable Soups

White Vegetable Stock
Brown Vegetable Stock
American Vegetable Soup
Asparagus Soup
Artichoke Soup
Avocado Soup
Cabbage and Apple Soup
Carrot Soup
Cauliflower or Broccoli Soup
Celery Soup
Celery Root Soup
Eggplant Soup
Escarole Soup
Fennel Soup
Garlic Soup

Gazpacho Blanco
Jerusalem Artichoke Soup
Lentil Soup
Mushroom Soup
Mushroom-Barley Soup
Okra Soup
Parsnip Soup
Pea and Ginger Soup
Rutabaga Soup
Spinach and Quail Egg Soup
Tomatillo Soup
Tomato-Saffron Soup
White Asparagus and Lemon
    Thyme Soup

VEGETABLE STOCK

Here are two vegetable stocks that are fragrant and full of flavor, good enough to serve as low-calorie consommés or with last-minute additions of rice, herbs or bits of vegetables. Vegetarians will find them useful in any recipe that calls for chicken or meat stock. The brown is hearty enough to use in place of beef stock; the white is more delicate. You can use either in place of the water in the recipes that follow.

WHITE VEGETABLE STOCK

1 leek, white part only,
*   chopped*
1 large Spanish onion, chopped
3 stalks celery, chopped
1 parsnip, pared and chopped
1 white turnip, pared and
*   chopped*
1 whole bulb garlic, unpeeled,
*   cut in half horizontally*
Small head of lettuce,
*   preferably romaine, chopped*
*   (2 cups)*

1-inch piece fresh ginger, pared
*   and minced (1 tablespoon)*
12 parsley stems, cut in 1-inch
*   lengths (½ cup)*
3 sprigs fresh thyme or
*   ½ teaspoon dried thyme*
1 sprig fresh rosemary or
*   ¼ teaspoon dried rosemary*
12 black peppercorns
4 quarts cold water
2 teaspoons coarse salt

Place the vegetables in a large stockpot. If you are using dried herbs, crush them between your fingers before adding to the pot. Crack the peppercorns into the pot. Pour in the water and salt and bring to a boil. Lower the heat and simmer, partially covered, for about 1 hour, or until all the vegetables are quite soft. Pour the soup through a colander set over another container, pressing the vegetables against the sides of the colander to extract their juices, then discarding the solids. Pour the broth through a strainer lined with a napkin or cheesecloth. Cool and refrigerate.

BROWN VEGETABLE STOCK

2 tablespoons olive or
   vegetable oil
2 large onions, unpeeled, sliced
2 large carrots, pared and
   chopped
2 sprigs fresh thyme or
   ½ teaspoon dried thyme
1 sprig fresh rosemary or
   ¼ teaspoon dried rosemary
2 whole cloves

2 bay leaves
12 black peppercorns
3 fresh or canned plum
   tomatoes, chopped
1 white turnip, pared and
   chopped
1 whole bulb garlic, unpeeled,
   cut in half horizontally
3½ quarts cold water
2 teaspoons coarse salt

In a heavy skillet, heat the oil and cook the onions over moderate heat for 10 to 15 minutes, or until they have begun to soften and brown. Add the carrots and cook the vegetables together another 10 to 15 minutes, stirring occasionally until they are as brown as possible without burning. Stir in the thyme, rosemary, cloves, bay leaves and peppercorns, remembering to crush the dried herbs between your fingers and crack the peppercorns. Add the tomatoes and stir well. Transfer the ingredients to a larger pot, scraping up all the browned bits on the bottom of the skillet.

Add the turnip, garlic, cold water and salt. Bring to a boil, lower the heat and let simmer, partially covered for about 1 hour, or until all the vegetables are very soft. Remove the pot from the stove and pour the contents through a colander set over a large container, mashing the vegetables against the sides to extract all the juices and discarding the solids. Strain a second time through a strainer lined with a napkin or cheesecloth, and discard anything that collects in the cloth. Cool and refrigerate the stock.

(If you like, you can simply let the vegetables drain once in a cheesecloth-lined colander set over a container. The result will be a slightly less intense flavor, but the stock will have a greater clarity.)

AMERICAN VEGETABLE SOUP

An uncommon combination of vegetables from the American continents: peppers, of course, which originated in this hemisphere; yuca, not well known in North America, but widely used in Caribbean and South American cooking; and hominy—not the Southern breakfast food but whole white corn kernels you can buy in cans—for which the Spanish word is *mote*.

¼ cup olive or vegetable oil
2 large onions, chopped
* (2 cups)*
1 tablespoon minced garlic
1 teaspoon minced ginger
1 teaspoon chopped fresh
* thyme or ¼ teaspoon dried*
* thyme*
¼ teaspoon ground cumin
3 stalks celery, diced
1 medium carrot, diced
8 cups water
2 teaspoons coarse salt
2½ cups yuca cut in ¾-inch
* cubes*

¼ pound string beans, cut in
* 1-inch pieces on the diagonal*
2 sweet red peppers, seeded
* and diced*
1 cup cooked or canned hominy
* (white corn kernels)*
½ teaspoon white pepper

Garnish:
* ½ cup chopped basil or*
*   Italian parsley*
* Freshly grated Parmesan*
*   cheese*

Heat the oil in a large saucepan. Stir in the onions, garlic and ginger and sauté over medium heat until the onions turn light brown. Stir in the thyme and cumin and sauté for another minute. Add the celery and carrots and stir for 2 minutes. Turn off the heat.

While these vegetables are cooking, fill another pot with water, add salt and bring to a boil. Add the yuca and boil for 5 to 7 minutes. At this point the yuca will be slightly undercooked, like an underdone boiled potato. Scrape the onion mixture into the pot with the water and cook, covered, for about 10 minutes, or until the carrots and yuca are soft but not tender. Add the string beans, red peppers and hominy to the soup and simmer for 5 to 10 minutes more, or long enough for the beans and peppers to soften but not lose their bright color. Turn off the heat, add pepper and salt to taste.

To serve, ladle into heated soup bowls and garnish with herbs and grated cheese.

NOTE: Yuca is available frozen, which makes an acceptable substitute. If you buy fresh yuca and have some left over, wrap it tightly in a plastic bag and put it in the freezer until you need it again.

ASPARAGUS SOUP

Use any size asparagus, from pencil-thin reeds to big thick jumbos, but remember that the thicker the stalk is, the heavier its skin will be. It's wise to pare the stems before you cook them. By blanching the garnishing vegetables in the water that will be used for the soup, we are actually making a quick stock, a trick that doesn't let one bit of flavor or texture go to waste.

2 pounds asparagus
3 medium potatoes
8 cups water
2 teaspoons coarse salt
2 tablespoons butter
1 large onion, chopped
1 teaspoon minced garlic
1 teaspoon chopped fresh ginger, packed tight

2 sprigs fresh tarragon or
  ¼ teaspoon dried tarragon
⅛ teaspoon ground mace
¼ teaspoon sugar
1 tablespoon gin
¼ teaspoon white pepper

Cut off the tips of the asparagus and cut them into 1-inch lengths. Wash, drain and set aside. Chop the remaining stalks, first paring away the tough skins with a vegetable peeler. Drop the asparagus into a bowl of water. Pare the potatoes and cut enough of them into ½-inch cubes to make 2 cups. Fill a large saucepan with water and salt. Bring to a boil and drop in the potato cubes. Cook until done. Quarter and slice the rest of the potatoes and place in a bowl of cold water. When the potato cubes are soft but not mushy, remove them from the water with a slotted spoon and place in a small bowl of cold water. Then drop the reserved asparagus tips—*only the tips*—into the cooking water and blanch for 1 minute. Remove with a slotted spoon and drop into a bowl of cold water. (The tips and potato cubes will be last-minute additions to the cooked soup.) Reserve the pot of cooking water.

In another saucepan, heat the butter and sauté the onion, garlic and ginger over moderate heat for 5 to 10 minutes. Stir in the tarragon and mace and then add the sugar and gin, cooking for about 2 minutes, or until the gin cooks away. Transfer the contents of the saucepan to the other pot (with the water) and bring back to a boil. Drain the *sliced* potatoes and asparagus *stalks* and add to the pot. When the liquid returns to the boil, lower the heat, partially cover and cook for another 10 to 15 minutes, or until the vegetables are tender. Purée the soup in a blender or food processor until it is very smooth, then season to taste with white pepper and salt.

To serve, reheat with the reserved potato cubes and asparagus tips. Or, for a more colorful presentation, heat only the potatoes in the soup and the asparagus tips separately in boiling water. Drain and dry the tips. After filling heated soup bowls with soup, add the tips, which will float on the top, making a dark-green contrast to the pale-green soup.

ARTICHOKE SOUP

The artichoke belongs to the same family as the sunflower. Large or small, with pointed or rounded leaves, all artichokes have a rich, full perfume. Scraping the meat from the leaves, as you do in this recipe, is easier than it sounds. After you cook the artichokes, just pull off the leaves. Hold each one down by its tip and scrape out the meat with a teaspoon or with the side of a butter knife.

6 large artichokes, about
   10 ounces each
8 quarts water
½ lemon
2 tablespoons butter
2 tablespoons vegetable oil
2 medium onions, chopped
   (1 cup)
⅛ teaspoon dried tarragon

1 teaspoon sweet vermouth
2 teaspoons coarse salt
¼ teaspoon white pepper
¼ cup heavy cream (optional)

Garnish:
  2 tablespoons chopped dill or
    Italian parsley

Trim off the tough outer leaves from the artichokes. Snap off and discard the stems. Put in a large stockpot with the water and lemon and bring to a boil. The artichokes will bob about; it's wise to drape a towel or cheesecloth over them, tucking it carefully inside the pot, and put a weight on the cloth. Cook for 45 minutes to 1 hour, or until tender. Lift out with tongs and drain upside down in a colander. Reserve the cooking water.

When the artichokes are cool, pull off the leaves and scrape the meat from each one. Place the meat in a bowl. Trim the artichoke bottoms (hearts), removing and discarding the chokes. When all the artichokes are prepared, quarter three of the bottoms and set them aside. Mash the three remaining bottoms into the scraped meat.

In a saucepan, heat the butter and oil and cook the onion until it is translucent. Stir in the tarragon and vermouth and cook rapidly for about 2 minutes, or until the vermouth evaporates. Add 5 cups of the reserved cooking liquid with salt and white pepper. Bring to a boil, lower the heat and cook gently for 15 to 20 minutes. Remove from the heat and purée the soup in a blender until very smooth.

To serve, reheat in a double boiler, adding the cream if you like. Correct the seasoning. Ladle into heated soup bowls, adding the chunks of artichoke bottoms to each bowl and sprinkling with dill or parsley.

AVOCADO SOUP

The avocado, a staple food in Central and South America, is so neutral in flavor that we use it in sweet sorbets as well as in peppery guacamole. When an avocado pear is ripe, it has a loose skin and soft, buttery pulp. You can make an instant soup from it by puréeing the raw fruit, loosening it with chicken broth and seasoning with salt and pepper; be sure to add some lemon juice to preserve the clear green color. Here is a somewhat more elaborate recipe.

3 ripe avocados, about 9 ounces each
Juice of 1 lemon
4 tablespoons butter
1 clove garlic, minced
1 hot green jalapeño pepper, split, seeded and chopped, or ¼ teaspoon cayenne pepper
1 large onion, chopped (2 cups)
3 stalks celery, chopped (¾ cup)
1 tablespoon chopped fresh tarragon leaves or ½ teaspoon dried tarragon

¼ teaspoon dried cumin
⅛ teaspoon mace
2 scant tablespoons flour
6 cups water
2 teaspoons coarse salt
½ teaspoon white pepper

Garnish:
1 large red bell pepper, seeded and diced
Fresh basil, mint, dill or Italian parsley

Peel the avocados, cut in half, discard the pits and drop the halves into cold water to which you have added ½ teaspoon of the lemon juice.

In a saucepan, heat the butter and sauté the garlic and jalapeño pepper. Add the chopped onion and celery and sauté over moderate heat until the onion is translucent. Add the tarragon, cumin and mace and stir for a minute before mixing in the flour. Cook over medium heat for 2 minutes, making sure the flour and butter are totally blended. Add the water and salt, bring to a boil, lower the heat and simmer for 10 minutes. Remove from the heat and let cool.

Select and reserve the most attractive avocado half to use as a garnish. Cut up the remaining halves into coarse chunks and add to the now-cooled soup stock. Purée in a blender or food processor until smooth, adding the remaining lemon juice, the white pepper and more salt if necessary.

To serve hot, reheat in a double boiler and, just before you are ready to eat, cut the reserved avocado into thin slices and add to the soup. Ladle into heated bowls and sprinkle with diced red pepper and whole-leaf herbs, about ¼ teaspoon for each serving.

To serve cold, stir in the thinly sliced avocado and then chill thoroughly, covered with plastic wrap. Pour into chilled bowls and garnish as described above.

CABBAGE AND APPLE SOUP

The hearty flavor of cabbage becomes stronger as it cooks. To complement it, we add spices, sugar, or—as we did here—fruit. Green cabbage is widely available and has a dominant taste; red cabbage will taste the same but will alter the color of the soup; Savoy cabbage has a more delicate taste and more tender leaves than the others.

*Small head cabbage, about
 1¼ pounds*
6 tablespoons butter
1 large onion, sliced thin
1 clove garlic, minced
*3 green apples, pared, seeded
 and diced*
1 tablespoon sugar
½ teaspoon ground allspice

*2 teaspoons sherry or
 wine vinegar*
1 cup sweet vermouth
9 cups boiling water
2 teaspoons coarse salt
¼ teaspoon white pepper

Garnish:
 *2 tablespoons
  chopped dill*

Remove and discard any discolored outside leaves of the cabbage. Cut the cabbage into quarters. Remove and discard the hard core, and slice the leaves as thinly as possible. Drop the slices into a bowl of cold water and set aside.

In a saucepan, heat the butter and sauté the onion and garlic until the onion is golden. Add the apples, stirring for 1 minute, and then the sugar, tossing to coat the apples. Stir in the allspice and sherry or vinegar, lower the heat and sauté for about 5 minutes, or until the apples soften. Add the vermouth and cook until it nearly evaporates. Drain and shake dry the cabbage and combine with the other ingredients in the pan, cooking until it begins to wilt. Add water and salt, bring to a boil, lower the heat and simmer for about 40 minutes, or until the cabbage is tender to the bite. Remove from the heat and add white pepper and salt to taste.

To serve, ladle into heated soup bowls and garnish with chopped dill.

CARROT SOUP

Carrots are related to parsnips, fennel, celery, parsley and, even, to Queen Anne's lace. They range from tiny baby ones to huge woody horse carrots; the best are orange-yellow in color, short to medium in length and have undeveloped cores.

1½ pounds carrots	½ teaspoon dried savory
1 medium potato	¼ teaspoon mace
2 tablespoons butter	6 cups water
3–4 leeks, white part only, chopped (2 cups)	2 teaspoons coarse salt
1 teaspoon minced garlic	2 teaspoons Pernod
1 teaspoon chopped ginger	¼ teaspoon white pepper

Scrape the carrots, then slice a few of them into 2-inch julienne until there is enough to fill 2 cups. Drop into ice water and reserve. Chop the remaining carrots and set aside. Pare, quarter and slice the potato. Drop into cold water and set aside.

In a saucepan, heat 1 tablespoon butter and sauté the leeks, garlic and ginger for 5 minutes, or until the leeks soften. Then stir in the savory and mace and cook 1 minute before adding the *chopped* carrots. Cook 5 minutes, stirring once or twice. Add water and salt to the pot. Drain the potato slices and add them to the pot. Bring to a boil, lower the heat and simmer, covered, for 10 to 15 minutes, or until vegetables are soft. Remove from the heat and purée in a blender or food processor.

To prepare the garnish, drain the julienned carrots and pat dry. Melt the remaining tablespoon of butter in a small sauté pan. When it is hot, sauté the carrots briskly for about 2 minutes. Then add the Pernod, sprinkle with pepper and more salt and sauté another minute. Scrape into the puréed soup.

To serve, reheat in a double boiler, correct the seasoning and ladle into heated bowls.

CAULIFLOWER OR BROCCOLI SOUP

Cauliflower and broccoli belong to the cabbage family. Both have stalks that add thickening to a soup; both have superb flavor when cooked to the proper point, just long enough to tenderize them. With broccoli, you know you're all right as long as the color stays bright green. With cauliflower you'll have to keep poking at the base with a fork.

*About 2 pounds cauliflower or
   broccoli*
6 cups water
2 teaspoons salt
3 tablespoons butter
1 large onion, chopped
1 leek, white part only, chopped
1 teaspoon minced garlic
1 teaspoon chopped ginger
*½ teaspoon finely chopped
   hot green pepper or
   few drops Tabasco*

¼ teaspoon nutmeg
*Few tablespoons heavy cream
   (optional)*

Garnish:
   *2 tablespoons coarsely
      chopped Italian parsley*

Cut away the leaves and then quarter the cauliflower, discarding the hard core. Break off the florets, cut off the stems, drop the florets into cold water and peel the tough skin from the stems. Chop and reserve the stems. Do exactly the same if you are using broccoli.

Bring the water to a boil with the salt. Drop three or four of the most attractive florets in the water and blanch for 2 minutes. Remove with a slotted spoon and reserve for garnish. In a saucepan, heat the butter and sauté the onion, leek, garlic, ginger and hot pepper or Tabasco. Cook for 10 minutes, or until the onion is soft but not browned. Stir in the nutmeg and chopped cauliflower or broccoli stems and cook for 3 minutes. Drain the florets and add to the pan. Toss to coat with the onion mixture. Transfer the vegetables to the pot of blanching water and bring to a boil. Lower the heat and cook 10 to 15 minutes, partially covered, or until the vegetables are barely tender. Remove from the heat and purée in a blender or food processor, adding salt to taste.

To serve, reheat in a double boiler. Drain the blanched florets, cut them into tiny florets and put a few on each serving with a sprinkling of chopped parsley. To serve cold, chill completely, check again for salt, then stir in a few tablespoonsful of heavy cream to thin the soup and garnish as above.

CELERY SOUP

Celery is really three vegetables. The leaves, like parsley, make a garnish; the stalks, like asparagus, are flavorful but stringy; the heart, like a parsnip, is soft, aromatic and basic to most stocks. This soup, wonderful hot or cold, uses all parts of the celery.

1 large bunch celery	*¼ teaspoon nutmeg*
1 medium potato	*⅛ teaspoon ground anise*
4 tablespoons butter	*⅛ teaspoon dried thyme*
1 medium onion, chopped	*6 cups water*
1 clove garlic, minced	*2 teaspoons coarse salt*

Cut off and discard the tough root end, and then wash the celery. Drain and reserve three of the crispest inner stalks, with their tops, for garnish. Scrape the remaining stalks and chop them and the heart coarsely. Set aside. Pare and dice the potato, drop in cold water and set aside.

In a heavy saucepan, heat the butter and sauté the onion and garlic until the onion softens. Stir in the nutmeg, anise and thyme and cook for 1 minute. Then add the chopped celery, toss to coat with the butter and sauté for 3 minutes. Add the water, salt and diced potato and bring to a boil. Lower heat and simmer for 15 to 20 minutes, or until the celery and potatoes are soft. While the soup is cooking, prepare the garnish.

Cut the reserved celery stalks into 2-inch lengths, then slice into the thinnest possible julienne. Drop the julienne into ice water, where it will crisp and curl up. Cut the feathery, pale-green celery leaves into tiny bouquets. When the soup is finished, purée in a blender or food processor and correct the seasoning.

To serve, reheat in a double boiler and garnish each serving with a few curled julienne strips and diminutive celery-leaf clusters.

CELERY ROOT SOUP

Celery root, or celeriac, is a variety of celery grown for its root rather than its stalks. It is sweeter, earthier, and has a stronger bouquet than garden-variety celery, and is starchy enough to thicken a soup. Serve this soup hot or cold, but if you chill it, be sure to add extra seasoning. Cooks will tell you that the refrigerator eats salt.

1 medium onion, chopped
1 clove garlic, minced
1 hot pepper, seeded
⅛ teaspoon mace
1½ pounds celery root
7 cups water
3 tablespoons butter

2 teaspoons coarse salt
¼ teaspoon white pepper

Garnish:
½ cup sour cream
¼ cup chopped Italian parsley

In a saucepan, heat the butter and cook the onion, garlic and pepper, stirring frequently, until the onion is translucent. Stir in the mace. Pare and thinly slice the celery root. Cut off the stems and tie them together. Add to the saucepan with the water and salt. Bring to a boil and simmer for 25 minutes, or until the celery root is tender. Remove from the heat, discard the hot pepper and stems and purée the soup in a blender or food processor. Correct the seasoning with salt and pepper.

To serve, reheat in a double boiler. Pour into heated soup plates and garnish with a dollop of sour cream and a sprinkling of chopped parsley.

EGGPLANT SOUP

Eggplant has a subtle flavor that can turn bitter with rough treatment, but when it is roasted and peeled as it is in this soup, it has a very elegant and voluptuous quality. Large and small eggplants taste much the same, so you may as well use the larger ones for soup because they are easiest to peel.

3–4 medium eggplants
5 tablespoons olive oil
2 tablespoons dry sherry
⅛ teaspoon saffron
2 pounds tomatoes (4 or 5)
1 small carrot
1 large onion, chopped
2 cloves garlic, minced
1 bay leaf
½ teaspoon chopped rosemary
   leaves or ¼ teaspoon dried
   rosemary

6 cups water
2 teaspoons coarse salt
¼ teaspoon white pepper
¼ cup heavy cream

Garnish:
  2 tablespoons chopped
    coriander, mint or Italian
    parsley

Preheat the oven to 500°. Rub the eggplants with 2 tablespoons of the olive oil and prick each one in four or five places. While you wait for the oven to heat, combine the sherry and saffron in a small bowl and set them aside. Place the eggplants on a baking sheet and roast them for about 1 hour, turning them several times, until they collapse and the slightly charred skin pulls away from the body of the eggplant. Remove from the stove and let cool until you can handle them. Peel them by cutting into the skin near the narrow end and pulling it away in a downward direction. Skin one side, turn and skin the other. Halve the eggplants, then remove as many seeds as possible by scraping with a teaspoon. Reserve the eggplant halves.

Blanch the tomatoes in boiling water. Peel, cut into quarters and squeeze out the seeds. Chop the pulp. You should have a generous cup of tomato pulp. Set aside. Cut the carrot into fine dice and set aside.

In a large saucepan, heat the remaining 3 tablespoons olive oil and sauté the onion, garlic, bay leaf and rosemary until the onion is translucent. Stir in the sherry-saffron mixture and cook for another 5 minutes. Then add the carrot, stir, and add the tomatoes. Cook over low heat for about 10 minutes, or until the mixture thickens slightly. Chop the eggplants and add to the saucepan. Add the water and salt, bring to a boil, lower the heat and simmer for 5 minutes, or until all the vegetables are soft but not mushy. Remove from the heat, discard the bay leaf and ladle 1 cup of vegetables into a small bowl to reserve as a garnish. Purée the rest of the soup in a blender or food processor and season to taste with additional salt and pepper.

To serve, reheat in a double boiler, stirring in the cream at the end. Ladle into heated bowls and drop a small mound of reserved vegetables into the center of each serving. Sprinkle with fresh herbs.

ESCAROLE SOUP

You can use any lettuce for this soup: crisp romaine or iceberg, peppery chickory, delicate buttery Bibb or Boston. Each will add its own quality. All, however, have one thing in common. They cook quickly, almost as soon as they touch the hot water, and nothing is to be gained from cooking them longer.

2 pounds escarole
6 tablespoons olive oil
1 large onion, chopped
2 cloves garlic, minced
4 stalks celery, chopped (1 cup)
1 bay leaf
½ teaspoon ground mace
½ teaspoon dried thyme
2 teaspoons sugar
7 cups boiling water

2 teaspoons coarse salt
¼ teaspoon white pepper

Garnish:
  About 2 tablespoons olive oil
  2 cloves garlic, peeled
  6–12 pieces Italian bread in
    ½-inch cubes
  Grated Parmesan cheese

Prepare the escarole by stripping off the discolored outside leaves. Cut each head in half lengthwise, then in half again lengthwise. Lay the sections flat on a cutting board and cut crosswise at 1-inch intervals. Wash, drain and set aside. There will be a great volume of escarole, so choose a cooking pan that is wide. A large skillet would be fine.

Heat the olive oil and stir in the onion and garlic, cooking until the onion begins to be translucent. Stir in the celery and sauté for 5 minutes more. Add the bay leaf, mace, thyme and sugar, stirring for a minute or two over moderate heat. Add the escarole, a handful at a time. As the escarole collapses and there is more room in the pot, continue to add more, tossing it to mix with the other ingredients. When all the escarole is added and is beginning to soften, add the water and salt. Bring to a boil, lower the heat and simmer for 5 to 10 minutes. Stop cooking while the escarole is green and still has some bite. Remove from the heat, discard the bay leaf and season with salt and pepper to taste.

To prepare the croutons for the garnish, heat just enough olive oil to film the bottom of a large skillet. Less is better than more. Add the garlic cloves, slightly smashed, and when the oil is very hot, sauté the bread cubes on all sides. When the bread is all fried, drain on paper towels.

To serve, heat the soup to boiling. Ladle into heated bowls, add a few croutons and pass a bowl of Parmesan cheese to be added by each guest.

FENNEL SOUP

Fennel has a texture and appearance similar to those of celery, but it has a distinctive anise flavor. It can be eaten raw, baked or braised, but the best way to enjoy the flavor fully is by making it into a soup.

3 fennel bulbs
2 tablespoons butter
2 tablespoons olive oil
1 large onion, chopped
1 tablespoon chopped ginger
1 clove garlic, minced
½ teaspoon ground fennel
¼ teaspoon ground coriander
3 stalks celery, chopped
(¾ cup)

1 medium carrot, chopped
(¾ cup)
6 cups water
2 teaspoons coarse salt
¼ teaspoon white pepper
¼ cup heavy cream

Garnish:
Fresh dill

Cut away and discard any small shoots from the fennel bulbs. Cut the bulbs in half lengthwise, reserving some of the light-green feather tips for garnish, along with half of one fennel bulb. Chop up the remaining fennel, cutting out and discarding the cores. Set aside.

In a large saucepan, heat the butter and oil and sauté the onion, ginger and garlic until barely soft. Stir in the ground fennel and coriander. Sauté for 1 minute, then add the celery, carrot and chopped fennel and toss over medium heat for 5 minutes. The vegetables should still be firm. Add water and salt. Bring to a boil, lower the heat and simmer, covered, for about 15 minutes.

While the soup is cooking, prepare the garnish. Place the reserved half of a fennel bulb, cut-side down, on a flat surface. Cut in half lengthwise again. Discard the hard core and cut the fennel into very thin slices, dropping them into ice water (where they will curl like celery sticks). When the soup is finished, purée in a blender or food processor.

To serve, reheat in a double boiler, stirring in the pepper and the cream just before serving. Ladle into heated soup bowls and garnish each serving with the drained and dried fennel shreds together with a few feather fennel tops and/or fresh dill.

GARLIC SOUP

Garlic is a versatile vegetable, whose quality changes when it is chopped, sliced or used whole, when it is sautéed in oil, braised or eaten raw. You can even roast it and eat the warm buttery cloves as a vegetable. On nights when you think you have nothing in the kitchen to use for soup, you're sure to have a couple of garlic cloves and an egg: enough for this flavorful broth.

3 tablespoons olive oil
6 large cloves garlic, minced
1 bay leaf
3 tablespoons sweet vermouth
¼ teaspoon cayenne pepper
5 cups water
2 teaspoons coarse salt
6 eggs
White pepper

Garnish:
1–2 tablespoons olive oil
2 cloves garlic, peeled
6–12 pieces French bread,
  in ½-inch slices
¼ cup chopped Italian
  parsley

In a large saucepan, heat the olive oil, add the garlic and stir over medium heat until it is golden. It's very important not to allow the garlic to burn. Add the bay leaf, vermouth and cayenne and cook until the wine evaporates. Stir in 3 cups of the water and the salt and bring to a boil. Lower the heat and simmer 10 minutes. While the soup is cooking, break the eggs into a bowl, mix them with a fork, and add to them the remaining 2 cups of water. Remove the simmered soup from the heat and, beating with a fork, stir in the egg-and-water mixture. Return to the stove and heat, stirring constantly, *just to the point of boiling*. Do not let the soup boil, or it will curdle. Remove the bay leaf and season to taste.

The garlic croutons for the garnish can be made either in advance or at the last minute. In a large frying pan, heat the oil, add the garlic and just enough bread so that it is not crowded in the pan. Sauté on both sides, adding oil only if needed. Remove from the pan.

To serve, pour the hot soup into heated soup bowls. Top with one slice of fried bread and sprinkle with parsley.

GAZPACHO BLANCO

If you know gazpacho only as a thin tomato-based soup, gazpacho blanco, which is based on milk, almonds, garlic and olive oil, will come as a delicious surprise. The garnish? Seedless white *peeled* grapes. It seems a lot of work, but the soup is so quickly made and the effect so elegant, that you should make the extra effort.

12 ounces blanched almonds, ground to make 3 cups
5 slices white bread without crusts, ground to make a scant 2 cups
6 cups milk
2 cloves lightly crushed garlic, skin left on
¼ teaspoon cayenne pepper

1 tablespoon medium-dry sherry
1 tablespoon good olive oil
2 teaspoons coarse salt

Garnish:
½ pound seedless white grapes, about 2 cups

In a large glass, ceramic or stainless steel bowl, combine the ground almonds, bread crumbs, milk, garlic cloves (skewered with toothpicks for easy removal) and cayenne. Let soak for 20 minutes, or until the almonds and bread crumbs are quite soft. Discard the garlic and purée the mixture, a few cups at a time, in the blender. It will have a grainy texture. When the soup is all blended, return to the original bowl, cover, and let chill thoroughly: it should be very, very cold. To speed the chilling, you can place the bowl in a larger container that holds ice cubes, a little water and lots of salt.

While the soup cools, peel the grapes with a paring knife and refrigerate. When well chilled, stir in the sherry, olive oil and salt to taste.

To serve, bring the soup to the table in a cold tureen, with the grapes in a separate bowl. Ladle the soup into chilled soup plates—glass bowls are good—adding a handful of grapes to each serving.

JERUSALEM ARTICHOKE SOUP

This native American vegetable has a crisp texture like a water chestnut's when it is eaten raw; when it is cooked, it tastes a little like a globe artichoke. You may have seen it called a sunchoke. The skin is edible but not aesthetically pleasing, since it will color a purée gray. It should be removed before the vegetable is cooked.

6 sprigs fresh thyme or
  ¼ teaspoon dried thyme
3 cloves
12 white peppercorns, crushed
7 cups water
2 pounds Jerusalem artichokes
  (about 9 medium artichokes)

3 tablespoons butter
1 leek, white part only,
  chopped (½ cup)
1 medium onion, chopped
2 teaspoons coarse salt
¼ teaspoon white pepper

Tie the thyme, cloves and peppercorns in cheesecloth to make a bouquet garni. Put in a pot with the water, bring to a boil, lower the heat and simmer, while you proceed.

Pare the artichokes and cut three of them into julienne strips for the garnish. Drop these into a bowl of ice water: they will curl, as celery does. Cut the remaining artichokes into quarters, slice them and set aside. In a saucepan, heat the butter and sauté the leek and onion for 10 minutes. Add the sliced artichokes and toss for 1 to 2 minutes. Pour 6 cups of the simmering flavored water into the pot with the bouquet garni. Bring back to a boil, lower the heat and simmer for 25 minutes, or until the artichokes are soft. Remove from the heat and discard the bouquet garni, first squeezing it over the pot to extract all the juices. Purée the soup in a blender or food processor until it is very smooth and creamy. Season with salt and pepper.

To serve, reheat in a double boiler. Ladle into heated soup bowls and garnish each bowl with artichoke curls.

LENTIL SOUP

The difference between a simple soup and an elegant one can be the texture. If you want a velvety cream for a formal dinner, purée all the lentils. If you want a heartier, homelier soup, purée only about one-third of the lentils for thickening and leave the rest whole. And if you want a rustic but light soup, don't purée them at all.

1 cup dry lentils
3 tablespoons olive oil
1 medium onion, chopped
2 leeks, white part only,
* chopped (1 cup)*
1 clove garlic, minced
1 teaspoon chopped fresh
* thyme leaves or ¼ teaspoon*
* dried thyme*
¼ teaspoon ground cumin
¼ teaspoon ground bay leaf

3 stalks celery, diced (1 cup)
1 small carrot, diced (½ cup)
6 cups water
2 teaspoons coarse salt
White pepper

Garnish:
* 2 tomatoes, peeled, seeded*
*   and coarsely chopped*
¼ cup chopped coriander
* leaves*

Rinse lentils and soak in boiling water to cover while the other ingredients are cooking.

In a large saucepan, heat the olive oil and sauté the onion, leeks and garlic, stirring frequently, until the onion is golden but not browned. Stir in the thyme, cumin and bay leaf and cook for a minute. Add the celery and carrot, lower the heat and cook, covered, for 5 minutes, or until the vegetables begin to soften. Add the water, salt, pepper and drained lentils and bring to a boil. Lower the heat and simmer, covered, for about 1 hour, or until the lentils are soft and fully cooked.

To serve, purée all, part or none of the soup and ladle into hot soup plates with a tablespoon of chopped tomatoes in the center and chopped coriander surrounding the tomatoes.

MUSHROOM SOUP

Use any mushrooms you have in this soup. Obviously, wild mushrooms are the most flavorful: oak, shiitake, chanterelles or morels all would be spectacular, but ordinary domestic mushrooms are good, too. And if you add as little as ¼ pound of wild mushrooms to the homely champignons, their assertive flavor will upgrade the quality without raising the price too much. If you have some dried wild mushrooms, soak them and use them, and the carefully strained soaking water will add more flavor to the pot.

2 pounds mushrooms	*½ teaspoon white pepper*
6 tablespoons butter or oil	*2 tablespoons sweet vermouth*
1 large onion, chopped	*¼ cup flour*
1 leek, white part only, chopped	*6 cups water*
(½ cup)	*2 teaspoons coarse salt*
1 clove garlic, minced	*2 tablespoons heavy cream*
¼ teaspoon nutmeg	*(optional)*
¼ teaspoon ground thyme	

Wipe the mushrooms with a damp towel, reserving three of the most perfectly shaped and colored for a garnish. Chop the remaining mushrooms, stems and all, and set aside.

In a saucepan, heat the butter and sauté the onion, leek and garlic until the onion softens and turns golden. Add the nutmeg, thyme and pepper and cook 1 minute. Pour in the vermouth and cook until it evaporates. Add the chopped mushrooms and cook, stirring, over medium heat until they release their moisture and it evaporates. Then stir in the flour. The mixture will be very dry, and must be stirred patiently over low heat for as long as 10 minutes to develop the nutty taste of the mushrooms and intensify the brown color. Add water and salt and bring to a boil. Lower the heat and simmer for about 15 minutes, or until the mushrooms are tender but retain a slight bite. Correct the seasoning and remove from the heat. Slice the garnishing mushrooms paper-thin.

There are two ways to finish the soup. One is to serve it immediately in heated soup bowls, with a liberal amount of chopped parsley and

3 or 4 mushroom slices floating on each serving. The other is to purée
1 cup of the soup with the heavy cream, stir it into the soup as it reheats,
and serve with the same garnish.

MUSHROOM-BARLEY SOUP

This soup tastes as if it were made with beef stock, although it is actually
meatless. The barley adds to the meaty texture of the mushrooms; we
enhance the illusion by cooking the onions slowly until they turn a
rich, beeflike brown.

¼ cup pearl barley
1 pound mushrooms
2 tablespoons butter
2 tablespoons olive oil
2 large onions, cut in half and
   sliced thin
1 teaspoon minced garlic
1 bay leaf

3 tablespoons sweet vermouth
7 cups water
2 teaspoons coarse salt
¼ teaspoon white pepper

Garnish:
   ¼ cup chopped fresh
      coriander or Italian parsley

Cover the barley with water an inch above its surface. Boil for 2 minutes
and let rest in the water for 1 hour. Wipe the mushrooms with a damp
cloth and set them aside.

In a saucepan, heat the butter and olive oil, add the onions, garlic and
bay leaf and sauté over medium heat for about 5 minutes. Lower the
heat and continue to cook very slowly for 15 minutes more, stirring
frequently, until the onions turn a rich, dark brown. Don't burn them.
Stir in the vermouth and cook for 3 to 5 minutes, or until the vermouth
evaporates.

Quarter the mushrooms and add them to the pot. At first they will be
quite dry, but they will start to release moisture as you toss them over
the heat. Cook and stir for 15 minutes over medium-low heat. The
longer you cook them at this point, the richer the flavor will be. Drain
the barley and stir into the mushrooms. Add water and salt, bring to

a boil, reduce the heat and simmer, covered, for about 45 minutes, or until the barley is tender. Check the barley from time to time, and when it is cooked to your taste, turn off the heat, discard the bay leaf and add the pepper with more salt to taste.

To serve, ladle into heated soup bowls and garnish with chopped coriander or parsley.

OKRA SOUP

Okra comes from Africa, but is now identified with the cooking of New Orleans. Pick out the smallest okra pods in the shop so they can be left whole.

1 pound okra
6 tablespoons olive oil
1 large onion, chopped
1 teaspoon chopped ginger
1 teaspoon minced garlic
¼ teaspoon ground cumin
1¼ teaspoons oregano
1 bay leaf
¼ teaspoon sugar
2 tablespoons Amaretto liqueur
1 28-ounce can Italian plum
   tomatoes, put through the
   food mill, with water added
   to make 8 cups liquid

2 teaspoons coarse salt
¼ teaspoon white pepper

Garnish:
  2 tablespoons chopped
    Italian parsley
  Roasted sunflower seeds

To prepare the okra, cut the thinnest possible slice from the root end, being careful not to expose the seeds. Drop all the trimmed okra into a basin of water, then lift out and drain. Dry thoroughly.

In a saucepan, heat the oil just short of smoking and drop in the okra. Over medium-high heat, toss the okra in the pan to sear it for 2 to 3 minutes. Taste one—it should be firm to the bite. Drain in a colander set over a bowl to catch the oil. When it has drained for 5 minutes, return the oil to the frying pan, reheat and stir in the onion, ginger and garlic. Sauté until the onion has softened but not browned. Add the cumin, oregano and bay leaf and stir for 1 minute. Then stir in the sugar and Amaretto and cook until the liquid evaporates. Add the tomatoes and water and the salt. Bring to a boil, lower the heat and simmer, partially covered, for 25 minutes. The soup will thicken to a medium-rich consistency. Remove the bay leaf, add the pepper and correct the seasoning. Add the okra and return to a boil.

To serve, ladle into heated soup plates, garnish with parsley and sunflower seeds.

PARSNIP SOUP

Parsnips are related to carrots, but have a richer, sweeter taste. You can always use parsnips in place of carrots in a stock—in fact, the results will often be superior.

1½ pounds parsnips
3 stalks celery
4 tablespoons butter
1 medium onion, chopped
1 clove garlic, minced
1 bay leaf
¼ teaspoon nutmeg

¼ teaspoon dried thyme
6 cups water
2 teaspoons coarse salt
¼ teaspoon white pepper

Garnish:
  2 tablespoons chopped dill

Pare and chop the parsnips into ¼-inch dice. You should have about 4 cups. Scrape and chop the celery.

In a heavy saucepan, heat the butter and sauté the onion and garlic for 5 minutes, or until the onion begins to soften. Add the celery and sauté a few minutes longer. Add the bay leaf, nutmeg and thyme. Toss in the parsnips and stir for 2 minutes before you pour in the water with the salt. Bring to a boil, lower the heat and simmer until the parsnips are tender. Remove the bay leaf and purée the soup in a blender or food processor. Season with pepper and salt to taste.

To serve, reheat in a double boiler. Ladle into heated bowls and garnish with dill.

PEA AND GINGER SOUP

Fresh vegetables are usually best, but if fresh peas aren't young, small and thin-skinned, frozen peas can be better (just as canned tomatoes can be better than hard winter tomatoes). The peas in the soup make a complete protein when you eat them with bread. Always have bread on the table with soup. The neutral taste of French or Italian bread is good, but don't ignore tangy rye, dense black bread and rustic whole grains.

*2¼ pounds fresh peas or
    2 10-ounce packages frozen
    peas
3 tablespoons butter
2 large onions, chopped
1 leek, white part only, chopped
    (½ cup)
¼ cup minced fresh ginger
1 clove garlic, minced
2 stalks celery, chopped
    (½ cup)*

*⅛ teaspoon ground cloves
1 tablespoon chopped fresh
    tarragon or 1 teaspoon dried
    tarragon
6 cups water
2 teaspoons coarse salt
White pepper to taste*

*Garnish:
    Chopped fresh mint, basil or
        parsley*

Shell fresh peas and set aside. There should be 3 cups. If using frozen peas, defrost under cold running water, drain and set aside.

In a saucepan, heat the butter and sauté the onion, leek, ginger and garlic, stirring frequently, until the onion begins to soften. Add the celery and sauté until the onion becomes translucent. Add the cloves, stir once, then add the tarragon and cook 1 minute more.

In a separate pot, bring the water and salt to a boil. Add the *fresh* peas, and when the water returns to the boil, cook 1 minute. Remove ⅓ cup of the peas, drop into cold water and reserve for the garnish. If using *frozen* peas, reserve ⅓ cup, dropping the rest into the boiling salted water. Transfer the onion mixture to the pot with the peas and let all the ingredients cook together. Frozen peas will take about 7 minutes; fresh peas will take a little longer. When they are soft, remove from the heat and purée the soup in a blender until it is smooth and creamy.

To serve, reheat in a double boiler, adding white pepper and salt to taste. Ladle into heated soup bowls. Using the water in the bottom of the double boiler, quickly reheat the reserved peas. Drain thoroughly and add a teaspoonful to the center of each bowl of soup, then sprinkle the surface with the chopped herb of your choice.

NOTE: This can be served as a cold soup, thinned with a little cream and with the same garnishes added.

RUTABAGA SOUP

Rutabaga is a gutsy and dramatic vegetable with a strong personality, although many people think of it as ordinary. It is, of course, a variety of turnip, with a flavor and texture somewhere between a sweet potato and a radish.

*2 rutabagas, 1¼–1½ pounds
    each*
4 cups water
2 teaspoons coarse salt
*1 tablespoon olive or
    vegetable oil*
*2 slices bacon, cut in ½-inch
    pieces*
1 onion, chopped (1 cup)
1 teaspoon minced garlic
1 teaspoon minced ginger
*1 teaspoon seeded and chopped
    hot red pepper or*
⅛ teaspoon cayenne pepper

1 carrot, chopped (1 cup)
*⅛ teaspoon crushed caraway
    seeds*
5 cups Beef Stock (page 74)
*2 slices Jewish rye bread with
    caraway seeds*
1 cup milk
White pepper

Garnish:
    *⅓ cup chopped Italian
    parsley*

Pare the rutabagas and dice enough to make 2 cups. Set aside. Coarsely chop the remaining rutabaga. Heat the water to the boiling point, add salt and drop in the *diced* rutabaga. Boil for 3 minutes, or until they are soft but still crunchy. Drain and reserve both the diced rutabaga and the water in which it was cooked.

In a large skillet, heat the oil and cook the bacon only until it releases its fat. Do not let it brown. Then stir in the chopped onion and sauté for 3 to 4 minutes, or until it softens. Add the garlic, ginger, hot pepper or cayenne and stir over moderate heat for another 3 to 4 minutes. Add the chopped carrot, caraway seeds and the unblanched *chopped* rutabaga. Toss the vegetables in the skillet for 3 minutes, then transfer to a stockpot with the beef stock and the reserved blanching water. Cut the crusts from the rye bread, tear the slices into 1-inch pieces and add to the pot. Bring to a boil, lower the heat and simmer for 30 minutes, or until the vegetables are soft.

Remove the pot from the stove and let it cool slightly. Purée the contents in a blender in several batches. Then pour into the top of a double boiler, stir in the milk, add white pepper to taste and correct the seasoning. Reheat and, at the end, add the blanched diced rutabaga, cooking it just until it is warmed through.

To serve, ladle the soup into preheated bowls and garnish with chopped parsley. Serve with more rye bread and sweet butter.

SPINACH AND QUAIL EGG SOUP

Adding body and richness to the stock, eggs usually play a passive role in soup-making. Here, tiny and delicate-flavored quail eggs are poached and become the garnish of a richly colored soup. I can almost always get quail eggs in New York, but if you can't find them, use a single chicken or duck egg in each bowl of soup.

1½ pounds fresh spinach
5 tablespoons olive oil
1 large onion, chopped
4 cloves garlic, minced
1 teaspoon chopped ginger
⅛ teaspoon allspice
Scant ⅛ teaspoon cayenne
  pepper

4–6 cups hot water
2 teaspoons coarse salt

Garnish:
  6–18 quail eggs, or
  1–3 per serving

Remove and discard spinach stems. Wash the spinach leaves well. If they are large, cut into smaller pieces. Drain and dry thoroughly before using.

In a large frying pan, heat 4 tablespoons of the oil and cook the onion, garlic and ginger over moderate heat until the onion is barely soft. Stir in the allspice and cayenne and cook 1 minute. Add the spinach leaves, a handful at a time, tossing in the pan until the spinach wilts and makes room for more. Cook until all the spinach has wilted down. If your pan is large enough, add 4 cups of water and salt. Otherwise, transfer to a large saucepan. Add water and salt. Bring to a boil, lower the heat and simmer for 5 minutes. Depending on how much water the spinach has released, you may need to add 1 or even 2 cups water. Continue to simmer another 5 minutes. Do not overcook, or the spinach will lose its dark-green color. Stir in the remaining tablespoon of oil and remove from the heat.

To cook the quail eggs, first drop them, in the shells, into boiling water for 1 minute. Remove and break into a saucer as described in the Note below.

To serve, pour the reheated soup into hot soup bowls and place the eggs, one at a time, into each bowl. The hot soup will continue to poach the delicate eggs. Or poach the eggs out of the shells in a shallow pan of simmering water, then transfer them to the hot soup when ready to serve. This method is useful if you want to break and cook the eggs in advance.

NOTE: A hen's egg can be cracked easily, unlike a quail egg, which has a very delicate shell but a surprisingly strong and resistant membrane. The usual egg-cracking method just doesn't work. The following procedure sounds unorthodox, but once mastered it is the solution to cracking quail eggs.

Hold the tiny egg between the thumb and forefinger of your left hand if you are right-handed. With a small paring knife, pierce the shell on the long side and push the tip in and out through the upper quarter of the egg, keeping it as close to the shell as possible. The tip will emerge about half an inch from its point of entry. You can then lift off a piece of shell to create a window. Turn the egg upside down so that the contents slowly fall out the "window."

TOMATILLO SOUP

The tomatillo looks like a small green tomato, and is wrapped in a husk. It has a lemony flavor and is used in Mexico in making salsas. If you can't find any tomatillos, use unripe tomatoes instead.

3 pounds tomatillos or
   unripe tomatoes
¼ cup olive oil
1 onion, chopped
4 cloves garlic, minced
   (1 tablespoon)
2–3 fresh jalapeño peppers,
   seeded and chopped
¼ teaspoon ground cumin

2 teaspoons coarse salt
6 cups Veal Stock (page 73),
   Chicken Stock (page 105) or
   Vegetable Stock (page 3)

Garnish:
   2 ounces julienned ham:
     Serrano, prosciutto or
     Smithfield

If you are using tomatillos, remove their husks. Rinse and dry the tomatoes (or tomatillos) and set aside 1 pound of the smallest and firmest. Chop the remaining 2 pounds and set aside.

In a casserole, heat half the olive oil. Cook two-thirds of the chopped onion over moderate heat, stirring until the onion wilts. Stir in the garlic, peppers and cumin and cook for 5 minutes. Add the chopped tomatoes and salt and cook 3 to 4 minutes more.

In a separate pan, heat 3 cups of stock. Pour the hot stock into the tomato-filled casserole and simmer for 10 minutes, or until the tomatoes are thoroughly cooked. Remove from the heat, and when the mixture is cool enough to handle, pass it through the finest holes of a food mill. (If you don't have a food mill, purée the mixture in a blender and then force it through a fine sieve.)

Cut the reserved tomatoes in quarters, discarding the hard stem ends. Set aside.

Rinse and dry the casserole. Return it to the heat with the rest of the olive oil and the reserved onion. Cook the onion for 1 minute, then add the quartered tomatoes and toss for 2 to 3 minutes.

Meanwhile, heat the remaining 3 cups of stock and add them to the tomatoes, letting them simmer together for 3 minutes. Now add the strained purée and let the soup simmer for 5 minutes more, or until the tomatoes lose their hardness but are still slightly undercooked. Taste the soup for seasoning. It will be fairly hot, thanks to the jalapeño peppers, but it may need more salt.

To serve, ladle the soup into preheated soup bowls, dividing the tomato quarters among the servings. Garnish with the ham julienne.

TOMATO-SAFFRON SOUP

The tomato, a South American fruit, comes in many varieties, from florid beefsteaks to tiny cherries, from yellow through green through red. But lately the most useful variety has been the canned. Now that fresh tomatoes are picked hard and shipped long distances, you often get the best results with canned tomatoes—unless, of course, you grow your own or live near a farmers' market. Notice that this soup is made in two steps. You do the second preparation while the first bubbles away on the stove.

FOR THE SOUP "STOCK"
¼ cup olive or vegetable oil
1 large onion, chopped
2 cloves garlic, minced
4 sprigs fresh thyme or
  ½ teaspoon dried thyme
2 fresh sage leaves or
  ½ teaspoon dried sage
½ teaspoon ground cumin
2 tablespoons tomato paste
1 28-ounce can Italian plum
  tomatoes
2½ teaspoons coarse salt

TO FINISH SOUP
1½ pounds ripe tomatoes, plus
  1 yellow tomato for garnish
½ cup sweet vermouth
⅛ teaspoon saffron
3 tablespoons olive or
  vegetable oil
1 medium onion, chopped
  (1 cup)
2 teaspoons sugar
¼ teaspoons white pepper

Garnish:
  2 tablespoons chopped
  Italian parsley

To make the soup stock, heat the oil in a saucepan and sauté the onion and garlic for about 5 minutes, or until the onion softens. Stir in the thyme, sage and cumin and continue to cook until the onion is totally translucent. Add the tomato paste, the canned tomatoes, juice and all, and cook over low heat, breaking up the tomatoes with a fork. Simmer for 15 minutes, covered, stirring occasionally. Remove from the heat and press the contents through a food mill or a strainer to extract all the liquid. Measure this stock and add enough water to make 6 cups. Stir in salt and set aside.

To finish the soup, blanch the fresh tomatoes in boiling water for 1 minute. Drain, peel and quarter them, and remove the seeds with a spoon. Chop the yellow tomato and set aside to use for the garnish. Chop the red tomatoes coarsely. Combine the vermouth and saffron and set aside.

In a saucepan, heat the oil and sauté the chopped onion for 5 minutes. Then stir in the sugar and cook 1 minute more. Add the vermouth and saffron mixture and stir over medium heat until the vermouth evaporates and the onion, thanks to the saffron, turns a golden orange. Add the chopped red tomatoes and sauté for 5 minutes, or until the mass thickens. Stir in the now finished tomato stock, bring to a boil, lower the heat and simmer 5 minutes. Remove from the heat and add the white pepper.

To serve, ladle into heated bowls, placing chopped yellow tomato in the center of each bowl and surrounding it with chopped parsley.

WHITE ASPARAGUS AND LEMON THYME SOUP

In New York I can buy white asparagus from Mexico, which has a more delicate taste than the green kind but a hard woody skin that must be removed before you cook it. Lemon thyme is an herb popular in Vietnamese cooking. If you can't find it, use ordinary thyme and add a piece of lemon peel to your bouquet garni.

2½ pounds white or green
asparagus
6 sprigs lemon thyme or
¼ teaspoon dried thyme
3 whole cloves
6 peppercorns
1 hot green pepper
5 cups water
2 teaspoons salt
4 tablespoons butter

1 large onion, chopped
3 stalks celery, chopped
(¾ cup)
1 clove garlic, minced
¼ teaspoon ground cumin
¼ cup dry vermouth
¼ teaspoon white pepper
2 tablespoons heavy cream

Garnish:
Whole lemon-thyme clusters

Cut the tips of the asparagus into 1-inch lengths and set aside. Tie the lemon thyme, cloves, peppercorns and hot green pepper in cheesecloth to make a bouquet garni. Place in a saucepan with the water and salt and bring to a boil. Drop in the tips, blanch for 1 minute, then remove with a slotted spoon and set aside to use for the garnish. Let the water continue to simmer, covered.

Pare and chop the asparagus stalks. In a large saucepan, heat the butter and sauté the onion, celery and garlic for 5 to 10 minutes, or until they soften. Stir in the cumin and cook 1 minute. Add the vermouth and cook until the liquid evaporates. Stir in the chopped asparagus stems and sauté for about 2 minutes more. Ladle 5 cups of blanching water, with the bouquet garni, into the saucepan. Bring to a boil, lower the heat and simmer for about 15 minutes, or until the asparagus is tender; white asparagus may take longer. Remove the pot from the stove and discard the bouquet garni after squeezing it over the pot to extract all the juices. Then purée the soup in a blender or food processor until very smooth. Add the white pepper and correct the seasoning.

To serve, reheat in a double boiler and add the cream at the last minute. Heat the reserved asparagus tips in the water in the bottom of the double boiler. Drain. Ladle the hot soup into heated bowls and garnish with asparagus tips and miniature bouquets of lemon-thyme clusters.

Fish Soups

FISH STOCK

Making fish stock takes no time at all: it's like brewing tea. You simmer fish bones and vegetables just long enough to take the bouquet from them, so that when you are done you have a broth with the delicate odor of the sea. I give two recipes for fish stocks or fumets. Both can be made with fish skeletons or shellfish shells. Never, by the way, throw away shrimp, crab or lobster shells. Put them in the freezer in a plastic bag, and they will be there to toss in the stockpot when you need some fish stock.

FISH STOCK I

A simple, lightly flavored broth.

3½–4 pounds of bones, skin, heads without gills and scraps of any white, non-oily fish, such as sole, flounder or red snapper
3 cups chopped onions
1 medium carrot, chopped (¾ cup)
3 celery stalks and tops, chopped
1½-inch piece ginger, pared
1 bay leaf
6 sprigs dill
5 sprigs thyme or ½ teaspoon dried thyme
3 sprigs parsley
12 whole black peppercorns
1 tablespoon coarse salt
3 quarts cold water

Rinse and drain the fish and put in a stockpot with the rest of the ingredients. Bring to a boil, reduce the heat and simmer, uncovered, for 20 minutes, skimming off the scum that rises to the top. Remove from the heat and let cool slightly. Using a colander or fine sieve lined with cheesecloth, strain the stock. Refrigerate it, and when it is cold, remove any fat that has risen to the top.

FISH STOCK II

This is a more complex stock than Fish Stock I, and is especially good for soups such as bisques that need a rich, deep flavor. You can add a little sherry, chill it overnight and serve it congealed, sprinkled with plenty of fresh thyme, mint, tarragon or—my favorite—lovage.

6 pounds of bones, skin, heads
   without gills and scraps of
   any white non-oily fish, with
   shrimp, crab and lobster
   shells
1 large onion, chopped
1 large carrot, sliced
3 stalks celery and tops,
   chopped

12 whole black peppercorns
2 bay leaves
½ fennel bulb or fennel top or
   3 pieces dried fennel sticks
1 medium tomato, quartered, or
   2 plum tomatoes, halved
2 quarts cold water
2 cups white wine
1 tablespoon coarse salt

Proceed according to instructions for Fish Stock I (see preceding page).

A BONUS: When you have fish stock on hand, making a fish soup is no trouble at all. The simplest ingredients can be put together with surprisingly brilliant results.

4 tablespoons butter
12 medium garlic cloves
6 bass or flounder filets
Coarse salt

½ cup sliced basil leaves
6 plum tomatoes, quartered
2 quarts Fish Stock I or II

Heat the butter in a skillet and cook the garlic cloves until they are soft but not browned. Sprinkle the fish filets with salt and basil. Sauté for 5 minutes. Add the tomatoes and ladle on some soup. When everything is heated through, place 1 filet, 2 garlic cloves and 3 tomato chunks in each heated bowl and garnish with more basil leaves.

CHUPE

This is a substantial South American soup that is always made with milk, an obvious relative of North American fish chowders. To make it really Peruvian, you should use achiote oil to add the red-orange color and punchy taste. To make the oil (see below) you need annatto seeds. Paprika, which is easier to find, will add the necessary color but not the Peruvian flavor.

16–24 medium mussels
1 pound medium shrimp
1 pound bonito or striped
   bass filets
2 tablespoons olive oil and
   1 tablespoon achiote oil
   (see below); or 3 tablespoons
   olive oil and ½ teaspoon
   paprika
1 large onion, chopped
3 cloves garlic, minced
¼ teaspoon cumin seed
6 sprigs thyme or lemon thyme
   or ¼ teaspoon dried thyme
1 bay leaf

1 fresh green chile, seeded
   and diced
1 large potato, pared and diced
6 cups Fish Stock II
   (see opposite page)
2 teaspoons coarse salt
1 cup cooked fresh or frozen
   fava or lima beans
1 cup heavy cream or
   half-and-half

Garnish:
   2 tablespoons chopped
      coriander

Clean the mussels following the instructions for Mussel Bisque (page 54) and refrigerate. You may peel the shrimp except for the tails, but for the most authentic chupe, leave the shells on the shrimp. Refrigerate. Cut the fish filets into 2-inch pieces and refrigerate.

   In a saucepan, heat the olive and achiote oils (or the olive oil alone). Add the chopped onion, garlic and cumin seed, and if using olive oil only, add paprika. Stir in the thyme, bay leaf and green chile and sauté over medium heat for 5 to 10 minutes, or until the onion softens. Add the potato, fish stock and salt. Bring to a boil, reduce heat and simmer, partially covered, until the potatoes are tender but firm. Add fava or lima beans. Let the soup return to the boil, add the drained mussels and shrimp and simmer, covered, for about 3 minutes, until the mussels open and the shrimp turn red. *Do not overcook.* Drop in the pieces of fish to cook in the hot soup for 1 minute. Quickly stir in the cream or half-and-half and remove from the heat just before the soup returns to the boil.

To serve, remove the mussels and shrimp with tongs and the fish with a slotted spoon. Divide among heated soup plates, ladle on the broth and sprinkle with chopped coriander.

ACHIOTE OIL

¾ cup annatto seeds   *1 cup vegetable or olive oil*
1 dried hot pepper, crumbled

Heat all ingredients in a small saucepan until the oil begins to bubble. Remove from the heat and let cool. Pour through a strainer lined with cheesecloth, squeezing the cloth and seeds to get out all the flavor. Achiote oil will keep in the refrigerator for up to a year.

CHUPE A LA AREQUIPEÑA

This recipe is a gift from my mother: colorful, easy to make and providing at least ten totally satisfying servings. Arequipa is the name of a town in the south of Peru. Each town on the coast has its own version of chupe, and the Arequipanians make theirs rich with milk, cheese and cream. Calabaza is a South American squash that you can find in Spanish markets, but you can use butternut squash instead.

½ cup vegetable oil
1 medium onion, chopped
2 hot chile peppers, seeded and
 chopped fine
4 cloves garlic, minced
¼ teaspoon oregano
1 large tomato, peeled, seeded
 and chopped
2 quarts plus 3 cups
 Fish Stock I (see page 39)
1½ tablespoons coarse salt
1 pound calabaza, pared, seeded
 and cut in ½-inch cubes
3 potatoes, peeled and diced
 (1 pound)
2 ears corn on the cob

1½ cups fresh peas or
 1 10-ounce package frozen
 peas
1 cup cooked rice
½ cup milk
½ cup heavy cream
¼ pound feta or ricotta cheese
¼ teaspoon white pepper
1¾ pounds flounder filets,
 cut in half lengthwise, then
 in 3 crosswise pieces each
1 cup flour, combined with
 1 tablespoon coarse salt for
 dredging
¼ cup vegetable oil for frying

Heat ½ cup oil in a large skillet and sauté the onion, hot pepper and garlic for about 5 minutes, or until the onion turns trauslucent. Add oregano and tomato and cook for 2 minutes. Pour in the fish stock and salt and bring to a boil. Add the cubed squash and potatoes and simmer at least 10 minutes, or until the potatoes are tender. While the soup simmers, cut one ear of corn into ½-inch rounds, and cut off the kernels from the other ear, discarding the cob. When the potatoes are cooked, add the corn, peas and rice to the soup and cook 3 minutes more.

Put the milk, cream and cheese in a blender and blend only long enough to combine. Pour the mixture into the simmering soup, stirring vigorously. Add the white pepper, correct the seasoning and keep at a simmer, covered, over very low heat.

Dredge the fish in the mixture of flour and salt. Heat ¼ cup oil in a large frying pan. When it is very hot, shake off the excess flour from the fish and fry until the coating is golden brown on both sides. *Do not overcook*: the fish should be fried in less than 5 minutes.

To serve, ladle the hot soup into heated bowls and place 3 or 4 pieces of fried fish in each one.

CRAWFISH BISQUE

Crawfish is one of the richest of shellfish. In this bisque, crushed whole crawfish give a fabulous flavor. If you can't get crawfish, you can substitute blue crab, lobster or shrimp.

⅛ teaspoon saffron
¼ teaspoon cayenne pepper
¼ cup sweet vermouth
2½–3 pounds crawfish
¼ cup olive oil
1 large onion, chopped
1 leek, white part only, chopped
* (½ cup)*
1 clove garlic, minced
1 heaping teaspoon chopped
* ginger*
2 large stalks celery, chopped
* (½ cup)*
1 medium parsnip, chopped
* (⅓ cup)*

3 sprigs Italian parsley, tied to
* 1 bay leaf*
4–5 tomatoes, chopped
* (2 pounds)*
3 cups cooked white rice
6 cups Fish Stock II
* (see page 40)*
2 teaspoons coarse salt
1 tablespoon sherry
¼ teaspoon white pepper
Coarse salt

Garnish:
* 2 tablespoons chopped thyme,*
* Italian parsley or dill*

Combine the saffron, cayenne pepper and vermouth in a small bowl and set aside. Remove about 1 pound of crawfish and refrigerate the rest. Pound and crush the shells and bodies of the pound of crawfish with a mortar and pestle. Set aside.

In a saucepan, heat 3 tablespoons of olive oil and sauté the onion, leek, garlic and ginger over moderate heat, stirring, for about 5 minutes, or until the onion turns translucent. Add the celery, parsnip, parsley and bay leaf and cook for about 7 minutes, or until the vegetables are barely tender. Stir in the saffron mixture and cook until the vermouth evaporates —a matter of a minute or so. Stir in the tomatoes, cover the pot and simmer over low heat until the tomatoes are soft, stirring now and then so the mixture doesn't burn. Add the rice, fish stock, crushed shells and bodies and salt and bring to a boil. Reduce the heat, cover and simmer for 10 minutes. Remove the pan from the stove, discard the bay leaf and parsley and as many of the shells as you can fish out. Put the contents of the pan through a fine sieve.

If a smooth bisque is desired, put the soup in a blender or processor and purée until it is silky-smooth. If you prefer a textured bisque, you can omit this step. Place the soup in the top of a double boiler and heat as you prepare the remaining crawfish.

In a skillet large enough to hold the crawfish without crowding, heat the remaining tablespoon of olive oil and sauté the crawfish for 2 to 3 minutes, shaking the pan until the fish turns bright red. Pour the now-hot bisque into the skillet, add the sherry, white pepper and salt to taste and bring to the boiling point.

To serve, fill heated bowls with crawfish and bisque and garnish with chopped herbs.

VARIATIONS: This bisque can also be made with shrimp, blue crab or lobster. Buy fresh shrimp with heads and tails, and follow the directions for crawfish. If you use blue crabs, remove the large oval shells and crush the rest of the crab with a mortar and pestle, adding the large shells to the stock. If you use lobster, crack the shells open, remove the tail and claw meat in large pieces, pound the shells and add to the stock. To finish, sauté the tail and claw meat in a little hot butter, cut them into large pieces and add to the soup at the end.

COD BISQUE

Cod is one of the most important food fishes in the world, but is most often eaten salted. Fresh cod is rather bland in taste, but becomes rich and flavorful when it is concentrated into a bisque. Here the thick soup is ladled over pieces of fried cod for an interesting combination of textures.

¼ cup olive oil
1 medium onion, chopped
  (1 cup)
1 leek, white part only, chopped
  (½ cup)
1 teaspoon minced garlic
1 teaspoon minced ginger
1 medium carrot, diced
6 stalks celery, diced
½ pound tomatoes, peeled,
  seeded and chopped (1 cup)
3 sweet red peppers, seeded
  and chopped
2 tablespoons sweet sherry

8 cups Fish Stock I
  (see page 39)
2 teaspoons coarse salt
1 cup cooked rice
3 tablespoons butter
3 tablespoons vegetable oil
⅓ cup flour
1½ pounds cod filets, cut into
  1- by 2-inch pieces
Coarse salt and white pepper

Garnish:
  ⅓ cup chopped Italian
    parsley

Heat the olive oil in a saucepan and sauté the onion, leek, garlic and ginger for 5 minutes, or until the onion begins to wilt. Add the carrot and one-half of the celery, reserving the other half. Add the tomatoes, lower the heat and simmer, covered, about 8 minutes. The mixture will become quite dry, so be careful not to let it burn. Add the peppers and sherry, cover the pot and cook for 5 minutes. Ladle in the fish stock, 2 teaspoons salt and cooked rice, bring to a boil, lower the heat and simmer, covered, for 10 minutes. Remove from the heat and, with a strainer, take out 1 cup of the vegetable-rice mixture to use as a garnish. Purée the rest of the soup with a food mill or in a food processor or blender. Return the purée to the saucepan with the reserved celery and correct the seasoning with salt and pepper to taste. Set over low heat as you prepare the fish.

In a skillet large enough to hold the fish without crowding, heat the butter and vegetable oil. Toss the pieces of fish in flour and add them to the hot butter and oil, shaking to move the pieces about. Turn to cook on both sides. Work quickly: the fish will cook in less than 5 minutes.

To serve, put pieces of fish in heated soup plates. Ladle hot soup over them and put a mound of the reserved vegetable-rice mixture in the center of each bowl. Garnish with chopped parsley.

CRAB-OKRA SOUP

Here crabs are cooked with okra in what seems to me a very Southern dish, although okra originated in Africa. You can even put a scoop of cooked rice in each bowl and make a kind of gumbo. The sorrel adds a lemony tang, and the beer, quite common in South American cooking, gives a rich undertone. This is not a soup for a formal party. It's casual and hearty, and you should use your fingers to pick out bits of crab from the shells.

10 large blue claw crabs
8 cups Fish Stock II
(see page 40)
1 large onion, chopped
2 stalks celery, chopped
(½ cup)
1 small parsnip or carrot,
chopped fine (½ cup)
5 sprigs dill
5 sprigs Italian parsley
1 bay leaf
3 whole cloves
3 tablespoons olive oil
1 clove garlic, minced

½ teaspoon dried red pepper or
chili powder
½ pound small okra, left whole
1 hot red pepper, seeded and
julienned
½ cup light-colored beer
2 teaspoons coarse salt
1 cup shredded sorrel leaves
(or spinach with a little
lemon)

Garnish:
1½ cups cooked rice
(optional)

Have the fishmonger cut the crabs straight down the middle, after removing the spongy white gills. Set half the crabs aside and chop the remaining 4 halves into small pieces (which will be used to enrich the stock).

In a large pot, heat the stock with half of the onion, the celery, parsnip or carrot, dill, parsley, bay leaf, cloves and chopped crab. Bring to a boil and simmer, partially covered, for 10 to 15 minutes, or until the vegetables are soft. Remove from the heat.

In a large saucepan, one with a lot of surface, heat the oil and sauté the remaining onion with the garlic and dried red pepper or chili powder for about 5 minutes, or until the onion is translucent. Add the okra and fresh hot pepper and toss in the pan for 2 minutes. Stir in the beer and cook until it evaporates. Then add the crab halves, tossing them for a minute or two, until the shells begin to turn color. Remove from the heat.

Strain the fish stock through a sieve or colander lined with several layers of cheesecloth. Squeeze all the juice you can from the crab and vegetables. There should be at least 6 cups of broth. Add the salt and pour the broth into the large pan with the crabs. Bring back to the boil, add the sorrel, reduce the heat and simmer a few minutes, just until the crabs turn bright red and the sorrel softens.

To serve, place 2 crab halves in each heated soup bowl with, if you like, a scoop of cooked rice. Divide the okra among the bowls and ladle in the broth and sorrel.

CURRIED HADDOCK SOUP

Haddock, a relative of cod, is a rather bland fish. Here it is enlivened by a curry-flavored broth. The curry-oil recipe makes more than enough for this soup. Keep the leftover oil in the refrigerator and use it as you might paprika: rubbed on chicken, added to mayonnaise or in savory pastries, such as empanadas. It takes 3 hours to make it, so allow plenty of time, or do it the day before you plan to make the soup.

Curry Oil:
  1 cup vegetable oil
  6 tablespoons curry powder
  ½-inch piece ginger, pared
  3 juniper berries
  1 cinnamon stick
  ½ teaspoon cayenne pepper
2 large onions, peeled and
  quartered
2 carrots, cut on the diagonal in
  ¼-inch slices (1½ cups)
1½ tablespoons tomato paste

2 tablespoons red wine vinegar
1 tablespoon light brown sugar
6 cups Fish Stock I
  (see page 39)
2 teaspoons coarse salt
1 large potato, pared and diced
  (1¼ cups)
1½ pounds haddock filets,
  cut into 2-inch chunks

Garnish:
  ½ cup chopped Italian
  parsley

To make the curry oil, combine the oil, curry powder, ginger, juniper berries, cinnamon and cayenne pepper in a small saucepan, bring to a boil, reduce heat and simmer very slowly for 2½ hours. Strain through a sieve lined with cheesecloth. Put the oil in a covered jar and place in the refrigerator, where it will keep for several weeks.

Heat 3 tablespoons of curry oil and sauté the onions and carrots in it until the onions turn translucent and the carrots begin to soften. Stir in the tomato paste, vinegar and sugar. Add the fish stock, salt and potato, bring to a boil, reduce the heat and simmer, partially covered, for 20 to 25 minutes, or until the vegetables are tender. Correct the seasoning and keep hot as you prepare the fish.

Dry the haddock. In a skillet large enough to hold the fish without crowding, heat 2 tablespoons of curry oil and sauté the haddock quickly on both sides. *Do not overcook.* The fish will be done in less than 5 minutes.

To serve, place some fish in each heated soup bowl and ladle the broth and vegetables over it. Sprinkle with parsley.

FLOUNDER SOUP WITH
TWENTY-FOUR CLOVES OF GARLIC

Don't worry about the twenty-four cloves of garlic: long, slow cooking makes them sweet, buttery and gentle on the breath. But be sure to allow enough time for this to happen when you make the soup, or cook the garlic early in the day and let it sit, covered, until you're ready to use it.

24 garlic cloves
6 tablespoons butter
6–8 flounder filets (1¼ pounds)
Coarse salt
½ cup sliced basil leaves

16 cherry tomatoes, blanched
and peeled
6½ cups Fish Stock I
(see page 39), heated

Blanch the garlic cloves in boiling water for 1 minute, then drain and peel. Place the cloves and butter in the top of a double boiler over simmering water. Cook gently for 1 hour, or until the cloves are soft. Set aside.

Lay the filets flat, skin side up, and sprinkle with salt and ¼ cup of the basil, reserving the rest for garnish. Then bring the wide ends of the filets to the tail ends, so that the soft side is outside. Place the garlic cloves and butter in a frying pan large enough to hold all the folded fish. As the butter heats, shake the pan so the garlic doesn't burn. When the butter begins to bubble, lower the heat and add the fillets, shaking the pan so that they don't stick. Cook only until they become firm: no more than 3 minutes. Don't turn them. Add the cherry tomatoes and the heated fish stock. Bring to the point of boiling, and correct the seasoning.

To serve, place a filet with 3 garlic cloves and a few tomatoes in each heated soup plate and then ladle on the broth. Garnish with basil.

HALIBUT SOUP

When halibut is treated this way, it has a delightful flavor and texture. You can make this soup with whatever white fish is freshest. I think you'll find the contrast of green soup and white fish flesh pleasing.

1½ pounds halibut
6 cups Fish Stock I
(see page 39)
2 teaspoons coarse salt
4 sprigs fresh tarragon or
½ teaspoon dried tarragon
1 medium potato, pared and
sliced thin (1½ cups)

2½ cups shelled fresh peas or
2 10-ounce packages frozen
peas
¼ teaspoon white pepper
4 tablespoons butter

Cut the halibut into 2-inch chunks and refrigerate.

Place the fish stock, salt, tarragon and potato in a saucepan. Bring to a boil, lower the heat and simmer, partially covered, for 10 minutes. Add 2 cups of peas, reserving the other ½ cup for garnish. Cook only until the peas are tender: 2 minutes for frozen, a bit longer for fresh. Remove the pan from the heat, discard the tarragon sprigs and let the soup cool slightly. As it cools, cook the reserved peas in a little salted water, then drain and set aside.

Purée the soup, cup by cup, in a blender until it is very smooth. Transfer to the top of a double boiler as you finish. Season with pepper and more salt, if needed.

In a skillet large enough to hold the fish without crowding, heat the butter until it bubbles. Quickly sauté the fish until it is lightly browned. *Do not overcook.*

To serve, place several pieces of fish into each heated soup bowl. Ladle on hot soup and drop a spoonful of the reserved peas in each bowl.

HERBAL FISH SOUP

An herbal soup with a slight taste of the sea. In summer you should be able to get fresh sorrel, thyme and mint. Fresh parsley, of course, is always available.

1 teaspoon butter
1 teaspoon oil
1 leek, white part only, chopped
  (½ cup)
1 cup chopped scallions
¾ pound shrimp, peeled,
  shells reserved
2 quarts Fish Stock II
  (see page 40)
2 teaspoons coarse salt
10 sprigs fresh parsley
8 sprigs fresh thyme or
  ¼ teaspoon dried thyme
8 fresh mint leaves
1 bay leaf
1½ pounds cod filets, in
  2-inch pieces

2 cups sorrel leaves,
  stems removed, cut crosswise
  (or spinach with a little
  lemon)
2 tablespoons chopped fresh
  thyme
½ cup chopped parsley
½ cup chopped chives
White pepper

Garnish:
  Lemon wedges

In a saucepan, heat the butter and oil and sauté the leek and scallions for about 5 minutes, or until they wilt. Add the shrimp shells and stir them about in the pan for a few minutes. Add the fish stock, salt, parsley sprigs, thyme, mint and bay leaf. Bring to a boil, reduce the heat and simmer, covered, for 15 minutes. Strain the stock through a sieve lined with cheesecloth, squeezing the vegetables to get out all the goodness. Return the clear soup to a saucepan and bring back to the boil before adding the shrimp and codfish. Reduce heat and simmer only about 4 minutes, or until the shrimp turn pink and the fish is barely cooked. Drop in the chopped sorrel, thyme, parsley and chives, add the white pepper, correct the seasoning and remove from the heat.

To serve, put 2 shrimp and a piece of cod in each heated soup plate. Ladle in the hot soup with herbs. Pass a bowl of lemon wedges, with seeds removed.

MARISCADA

A peasant soup that is served in the north of Peru, a light broth akin to a bouillabaisse. When I was a child, mariscada was just the start of a meal, but today it seems a substantial dish, a meal in itself with bread and some fruit. When you buy the clams, be sure they're tightly closed. If there's an opening, tap one side gently. In hard clams the shells should clamp together; in soft clams or steamers the neck should constrict.

18–24 small clams in shells, preferably littlenecks
18–24 medium mussels
6–8 crawfish, langoustine or large shrimp
12–16 sea scallops
¼ cup olive oil
1 medium onion, chopped (1 cup)
2 cloves garlic, minced
2 tablespoons chopped fresh thyme or lemon thyme or ½ teaspoon dried thyme
1 bay leaf

½ cup diced carrots
½ cup diced celery
3 pounds fresh plum tomatoes, peeled, quartered and seeded
½ teaspoon sugar
½ cup white wine
4 cups Fish Stock II (see page 40)
2 teaspoons coarse salt
White pepper

Garnish:
2 tablespoons grated lemon peel

Soak the clams in cold water and scrub to remove any sand. Put in the refrigerator in a shallow container. Clean the mussels following the instructions for Mussel Bisque (page 54). Both clams and mussels can be kept, cleaned, for several hours in the refrigerator.

Prepare the crawfish, langoustine or shrimp by stripping away the shells, except on the shrimp tails. Rinse, drain, cover and refrigerate.

Wipe the scallops with a damp towel and refrigerate.

In a saucepan, heat the olive oil and sauté the onion and garlic over moderate heat for 5 minutes. When the onions turn translucent, stir in the thyme and bay leaf, carrots and celery. Sauté for 5 minutes, or until the carrots soften slightly. Add tomatoes and sugar to the onion mixture and let it cook about 10 minutes, or until the mixture thickens. Add wine and cook for about 5 minutes, or until it evaporates. Finally add the fish stock and salt and bring to a boil. Remove the bay leaf, cover the pot and turn off the heat.

Put the clams, mussels and shrimp in a skillet large enough to hold them in one or two layers. Ladle on enough of the hot stock to cover. If the clams have not had time to relax in the refrigerator, put them in the skillet first, add the stock and give them a 5-minute head start before adding the rest of the shellfish. The shellfish is cooked when the clams and mussels open and the shrimp turn pink: 5 to 10 minutes. Watch them carefully, as overcooking will toughen them. Just before they are done, drop in the scallops, which will heat through and firm up in a minute. Add salt and pepper to taste.

To serve, work quickly so the soup will stay piping hot. Divide the shellfish among heated soup plates and ladle steaming soup over them. Sprinkle with grated lemon peel.

MUSSEL BISQUE

Buy fresh mussels in tightly closed black shells. Look for medium rather than large mussels, which can have too pungent a taste. In the past few years, cultivated mussels have come on the market. They are usually much cleaner than gathered mussels, and don't have to be scrubbed or soaked.

5 pounds mussels
1 cup white wine
3 tablespoons butter
2 teaspoons seeded and chopped
  fresh hot chile pepper
1 teaspoon minced garlic
1 teaspoon saffron threads,
  softened in ¼ cup
  medium-dry sherry
2 leeks, white part only,
  chopped (1 cup)
⅔ cup peeled and seeded
  tomatoes

1 small carrot, diced (½ cup)
2 medium potatoes, peeled and
  diced (2 cups)
½ cup heavy cream
Coarse salt
White pepper

Garnish:
  ½ cup chopped Italian
    parsley, basil or coriander

To clean the mussels, scrub them with a stiff brush to remove the dirt and "beard." Push your thumb against one side of the shell while you hold it in your hand. If the mussel is alive, as it should be, it will close up. The push may reveal there's no mussel inside, just a mass of packed sand. Throw it away, along with any mussels that remain open despite pressure to close them.

To help rid the scrubbed mussels of interior sand, put them in a pot and cover with cold water to which you add a small handful of flour or cornmeal. Let the mussels rest in the refrigerator for several hours or overnight. As they relax they will disgorge sand. When you're ready to cook the soup, lift out the mussels, leaving the floury water in the pot. For curiosity, look at the bottom of the pot to see how much sand has been released.

Put the mussels and wine in a large shallow pan with a lid. Cover the pan and steam the mussels over medium heat for 5 minutes, shaking the pan once in a while. When the mussels have opened, remove the pan from the heat. Discard any that have not opened. Remove the other mussels from their shells and discard the shells. Strain the liquid through a sieve lined with cheesecloth. There should be at least 3 cups of liquid. Add enough water to make 5 cups and set mussels and liquid aside.

In a saucepan, heat the butter and stir the chopped chile and the garlic over moderate heat about 3 minutes. Add the saffron-sherry mixture and cook until the liquid evaporates. Add the chopped leeks and cook until they soften. Then stir in the chopped tomatoes and carrots, forming a thick, dry mass. Pour in the 5 cups of mussel liquid, add the chopped potatoes and bring to the boil. Lower the heat and simmer, partially covered, for about 20 minutes, or until the carrots and potatoes are soft.

Remove the pan from the heat and let the contents cool slightly. Pick out twenty-four of the most attractive mussels, set aside, and add the rest to the soup. Purée the soup, cup by cup, in a blender to make a very smooth bisque. Strain the purée through a fine sieve to make sure no tough bits of mussel have remained. Put in the top of a double boiler, add cream and reheat to the boiling point. Drop in the reserved mussels and heat through.

To serve, ladle the bisque into heated bowls, with 3 mussels in each bowl. Sprinkle with chopped herbs. This is a very rich bisque, so portions should be small.

SALMON-DILL SOUP

Salmon and dill are a familiar combination, but you don't often find them in soup. Have the salmon cut in small steaks. If it's cut thinner, it would overcook and collapse in the broth. At one time salmon was plentiful along both North American coasts. Overfishing has nearly wiped out the Atlantic salmon, and now most of the salmon in the United States is sent by air from the Northern Pacific coast.

6 1-inch-thick salmon steaks
   (about ¼ pound each)
2 tablespoons butter
4 leeks, white part only,
   chopped (2 cups)
1 teaspoon minced garlic
1 bay leaf
3 tablespoons anise liqueur or
   ⅛ teaspoon anise seed
8 cups Fish Stock I
   (see page 39)

2 small potatoes, peeled and
   diced (2 cups)
2 teaspoons salt
Beurre manié:
   2 tablespoons soft butter
   2 tablespoons flour
½ cup heavy cream

Garnish:
   ½ cup finely chopped dill

Ask the fishmonger to cut the steaks from a small salmon, preferably from the tail end, and you will have the ideal size.

In a saucepan, melt the butter and sauté the leeks, garlic and bay leaf until the leeks begin to wilt. Pour in the anise liqueur and cook until it evaporates (or sauté the ground anise seed with the leeks.) Add the fish broth, potatoes and salt, bring to a boil, reduce heat and simmer, covered, until the potatoes are tender but hold their shape. Meanwhile, make a beurre manié by kneading together the butter and flour. Whisk bits of beurre manié into the hot soup, adding only enough to thicken the soup to your taste. You'll probably need all of it. Keep covered over a very low flame while you prepare the salmon.

Place the salmon steaks in a skillet large enough not to crowd the fish. Ladle on the soup, bring to a simmer and poach the fish for around 4 minutes, until the steaks turn opaque and become firm. *Do not overcook.*

To serve, transfer the salmon to heated soup bowls with a slotted spatula. Return the skillet to the stove, stir in the heavy cream and bring back just to the boiling point. Correct the seasoning and ladle the soup, dividing the potatoes evenly among the bowls. Sprinkle with dill.

SEA SCALLOP SOUP

Plump sea scallops puff up like dumplings in hot broth, while tender young bay scallops are best when least cooked, and should be added at the last minute, as though they were a garnish.

1½ pounds sea scallops
6 tablespoons olive oil
1 large onion, chopped
1 clove garlic, minced
1 fresh hot chile pepper, seeded and chopped
5 sprigs fresh thyme or ½ teaspoon dried thyme
1 bay leaf
1 carrot, chopped (½ cup)
2 stalks celery, chopped (½ cup)
3 cups drained canned Italian tomatoes

¼ teaspoon sugar
½ cup white wine
3 cups Fish Stock II (see page 40)
1–2 teaspoons coarse salt
¼ teaspoon white pepper

Garnish:
⅓ cup chopped Italian parsley or sliced scallions, or 2 tablespoons snipped chives

Wipe the scallops with a dry towel and put in a colander over a bowl to drain in the refrigerator. The scallops should be as dry as possible when you sear them later.

In a saucepan, heat 4 tablespoons of the olive oil and sauté the onion, garlic, chile pepper, thyme and bay leaf over moderate heat for 5 minutes, stirring frequently, until the onion begins to wilt. Add the carrot and celery, tomatoes and sugar, mashing the tomatoes with a wooden spoon.

Cover the pan and cook for about 10 minutes. Add the wine and cook, uncovered, for 5 minutes, or until it evaporates. The tomato base will be rather thick. Remove from the heat, discard the thyme sprigs and bay leaf and purée the mixture in a food mill set over a large saucepan. Return to the stove and add the fish stock and 1 teaspoon salt to the pan. Bring to a boil and lower the heat, correcting the seasoning with salt and white pepper.

Spread a dry dish towel on a counter and pat the scallops. In a large skillet, heat the remaining 2 tablespoons olive oil. When it is hazy, add the scallops, shaking the pan to keep them moving about. All sides should be seared but slightly raw inside after 3 minutes. *Do not overcook*: the hot soup will continue to cook them.

To serve, divide the scallops among the heated soup plates and ladle on very hot broth. Garnish with chopped herbs.

SHARK AND CHAMPIGNON SOUP

Despite its ominous name, shark has a taste and a texture like those of swordfish (which is a good substitute if you can't find mako). In Hawaii roast baby shark is considered a delicacy.

5 tablespoons olive oil
1½ cups chopped shallots
2 teaspoons minced garlic
1 tablespoon soy sauce
3 tablespoons sweet vermouth
½ pound mushrooms, sliced
6 cups Fish Stock I
  (see page 39)
2 tablespoons chopped fresh
  thyme or ¼ teaspoon dried
  thyme

3 tablespoons potato flour or
  2 tablespoons cornstarch
2 teaspoons coarse salt
2 pounds mako shark, cut into
  1- by 2-inch chunks

Garnish:
  ⅓ cup chopped Italian
    parsley

Heat 3 tablespoons of the olive oil in a saucepan and sauté the shallots and garlic until the shallots are golden. Add the soy sauce and cook 2 minutes, stirring frequently. Add the vermouth and cook until it evaporates. Add the mushrooms, stirring to combine with the other ingredients. (At first they will be very dry, but soon they will begin to release their liquid.) Continue to cook and stir over moderate heat until the mushrooms brown—at least 15 minutes. Then add the fish stock and thyme and bring to a simmer. Combine the potato flour or cornstarch with a little water and whisk it into the simmering stock with the salt. The soup will become slightly thickened. Cover the pot and turn off the heat.

In a large skillet, heat the remaining 2 tablespoons of olive oil. Dry the fish chunks. When the oil is very hot, sear the fish in the pan. Transfer to the pot with the stock and poach the fish over moderate heat until it is firm but not dry. *Do not overcook.*

To serve, add equal amounts of fish to each heated bowl and ladle on the soup and mushrooms. Sprinkle with parsley.

SHRIMP CHUPE

Another chupe, a hearty, flavorful soup not unlike a fish chowder. Large expensive shrimp look impressive, but soups are especially good made with tender tiny shrimp. Whatever size you use, never expose the shrimp to heat for more than 2 or 3 minutes.

2 pounds shrimp
6 cups Fish Stock II
* (see page 40)*
3 large potatoes
2 tablespoons butter
1 cup chopped shallots
2 leeks, white part only,
* chopped (1 cup)*

1 teaspoon minced garlic
4 sprigs fresh tarragon, tied
* together*
2 teaspoons coarse salt
2 tablespoons heavy cream
White pepper and coarse salt

Rinse and drain the shrimp, reserving four in their shells to use as garnish. Peel the remaining shrimp and chop their shells. In a stockpot, simmer the shells in the fish stock for 15 minutes. Strain the stock through a sieve lined with cheesecloth, discard the shells, and return the soup to the pot.

Add the shelled shrimp plus the 4 shrimp in shells to the pot. Bring to a boil, reduce the heat, and cook for 4 minutes, by which time the shrimp will be quite pink. Spoon out and dice the shelled shrimp. Put in one bowl, with the unshelled shrimp in another.

Pare and dice one of the potatoes and boil it in salted water until it is tender. Drain and set aside to add to the soup later.

In a saucepan, heat the butter and sauté the shallots, leeks, garlic and tarragon. Chop the remaining 2 potatoes. When the leeks begin to wilt, add the potatoes, the stock and 2 teaspoons salt to the pan and bring to a boil. Lower the heat and simmer for about 10 minutes, or until the potatoes are tender. Remove from the heat, discard the tarragon and add two-thirds of the diced shelled shrimp.

Purée this soup, cup by cup, in the blender until it is smooth and thick, pouring it into the top of a large double boiler as it is done. Heat in the double boiler, and when it is just at the boiling point, add the cooked diced potato and reserved diced shrimp. Continue heating as you stir in the cream, salt and white pepper to taste.

To serve, shell the four reserved shrimp and cut each in half lengthwise. Ladle the hot chupe with diced potatoes and shrimp into heated soup plates and float half a shrimp on each serving.

SOPA DE PEJERREY

Pejerrey means smelt, but you can use any small fish—fresh anchovies, sardines or whitebait—for this soup. Note that the fennel is not the familiar anise-flavored bulb, but dried twigs of wild fennel, the kind used to grill *loup au fenouil* in the South of France. The beer batter is best after a three-hour rest, so allow for that when you plan to make the soup.

Beer batter:
  ¾ cup flour
  Pinch of salt
  ¾ cup beer
1¼ pounds smelts (about 24)
3 tablespoons olive oil
1 medium onion, chopped
  (1 cup)
2 cloves garlic, minced
¼ teaspoon turmeric
⅛ teaspoon white pepper
3 tablespoons flour

7 cups Fish Stock I
  (see page 39)
4–6 fennel sticks
¼ pound Swiss chard
1 medium carrot, julienned in
  4-inch lengths
Coarse salt and white pepper
4 cups vegetable oil for frying

Garnish:
  2 tablespoons chopped
    Italian parsley or dill

To make the beer batter, place the flour and salt in a bowl and pour in the beer, stirring to combine thoroughly. Set aside for 3 hours at room temperature.

Ask your fishmonger to clean the fish, removing the guts, gills and spinal bones but keeping the heads intact. If you can, open the jaw of each fish and bring the tail through the open jaw and out through the mouth, pulling the tail forward as much as possible to create a triangular shape. Refrigerate.

In a saucepan, heat the olive oil and sauté the onion and garlic for 5 minutes, or until the onion softens. Stir in the turmeric and white pepper, then the flour, with a wooden spoon. The mixture will become quite thick. Gradually pour in the fish stock, whisking constantly so that it combines smoothly, without lumps. When all the stock has been added, put in the fennel sticks and simmer the soup, covered, for 10 minutes.

While the soup cooks, prepare the Swiss chard. Cut the crunchy white stems into 4-inch lengths and julienne them. Cut the dark-green leaves crosswise into ¼-inch-wide strips. Set aside.

When the soup has simmered for 10 minutes, add the carrot and cook 5 minutes more. Add the Swiss chard and simmer for a few more minutes, until the chard softens but keeps its dark-green color. Correct the seasoning with salt and white pepper, cover, and keep over low heat while you prepare the fish.

Heat the oil in a large heavy frying pan. Dip the smelts in the batter, taking care to coat each fish completely. When the oil is very hot, lift out the fish, one at a time, with your fingers, shake off the excess batter and drop into the hot oil. Do not crowd the pan. The fish is cooked when the batter turns golden brown. Lay the fish in a shallow pan lined with paper towels and place in a low oven.

To serve, ladle hot soup and vegetables into heated plates. Float three batter-fried fish on top of the soup in each bowl. Sprinkle with parsley or dill.

SOPA DE PULPO

Octopus is popular with Italians and Spanish-speaking people, but relatively unknown to most North Americans. It has a wonderful chewy texture. Some people think it should be cooked for days, but I like to use the contrast of hot and cold to tenderize it, as the Spanish do. I dip it into boiling liquid, remove it, dip it again and remove it again. Then I can simmer it for less than an hour, and it becomes marvelously tender.

1½ pounds octopus
7 quarts water
2 medium onions, peeled and
*   quartered*
2 celery stalks and tops, cut in
*   1-inch lengths*
1 carrot, diced
1-inch piece fresh ginger
8 garlic cloves
3 bay leaves
6 juniper berries

2 tablespoons coarse salt
2 tablespoons olive oil
⅛ teaspoon cayenne pepper
1 tablespoon Spanish paprika
¼ cup flour

Garnish:
*   1 tablespoon butter*
*   1 cup cooked or canned*
*   hominy (white corn*
*   kernels)*
*   1 tablespoon lemon juice*

Rinse the octopus under cold running water. Turn the mantle (it looks like a sack) inside out and clean it under running water. Place the octopus on your work table and sever the head just under the eye—or have your fishmonger prepare it for you.

To a stockpot filled with the water, add the onions, celery, carrot, ginger, 4 garlic cloves, 2 bay leaves, the juniper berries and salt. Bring to a boil, and holding the octopus by its mantle, lower the body and tentacles into the boiling liquid for a few seconds. Lift out and let cool as the liquid continues to simmer. When the octopus has cooled slightly, repeat the procedure and again set the octopus aside to cool slightly. After the second cooling, lower the whole octopus into the water and cook for 45 minutes, or until it is tender but chewy. Remove the octopus and reserve 6 cups of the cooking liquid, which will have turned a reddish brown.

When the octopus is cool enough to handle, hold it under warm running water and slice away the thick, dark skin. Leave the suction cups intact. Slice the mantle into 1-inch pieces and slice the tentacles into ½-inch diagonal pieces.

In a saucepan, heat the olive oil and add the remaining 4 cloves of garlic and the remaining bay leaf. When the garlic turns golden brown, remove the pan from the heat and stir in the cayenne pepper, paprika and flour. Return the pan to the stove and stir the mixture over low heat for 3 to 5 minutes before whisking in the reserved octopus stock. Whisk the soup until it is smooth and cook 5 minutes more. Remove the bay leaves. Add the octopus pieces to heat in the broth for about 3 minutes.

Prepare the garnish by melting the butter and stirring in the hominy and lemon juice. Divide equal amounts of octopus among heated soup plates. Ladle in the soup and garnish each serving with cooked hominy.

SQUID SOUP

Always buy fresh whole squid with clear skin and a light odor. Buy large squid: the bigger they are, the more ink they'll have. As it is, you'll have about ¼ teaspoon per squid, but it will be enough to turn the whole soup black. (If you can find only small squid without ink, you can buy fresh ink in Chinese fish markets, in which case you will need 1 or 2 teaspoons.) If you can't get any ink at all, the soup won't look as dramatic, but its taste won't be affected, since the squid's ink is a flavorless camouflage.

1½ pounds squid
 (4–5 large squid)
3 tablespoons sweet sherry
5 cups Fish Stock I
 (see page 39)
1 sprig fresh rosemary or
 Italian parsley
2 medium potatoes,
 peeled and diced (1½ cups)
3 tablespoons olive oil
1 large or 2 medium onions,
 chopped

3 tablespoons chopped
 coriander leaves
1 bay leaf
¼ teaspoon white pepper
Coarse salt

Garnish:
 1 sweet red pepper, seeded
 and julienned

Have the fishmonger prepare the squid, reserving the ink sac. Place the sacs (if you have them) in a strainer set over a cup and mash them with the back of a spoon to release the ink. Pour the sherry through the strainer, again rubbing with the spoon to capture every bit of the ink. Set aside.

Slice the cleaned bodies of the squid into rings no more than ¼ inch wide, and cut the tentacles into thirds. Put on paper towels to dry.

In a saucepan, heat the fish stock, rosemary or parsley and 1 cup of the diced potatoes. Bring to a boil, lower the heat and simmer for about 5 minutes, or until the potatoes are soft. Spoon out the potatoes, discard the herb and measure the stock. There should be at least 4 cups; if not, add more stock or water to make up that amount. Set potatoes and stock aside.

In a saucepan, heat 2 tablespoons of the olive oil and sauté the onions for 10 minutes with 1 tablespoon of the coriander and the bay leaf. Then stir in the uncooked ½ cup of diced potatoes and the ink-sherry mixture. Add the fish stock, bring to a boil, lower the heat and simmer for about 5 minutes, or until the potatoes are fully cooked. Remove from the heat, discard the bay leaf and let the soup cool slightly. Then purée, cup by cup, in a blender until it is very smooth. Add pepper and salt to taste and put in the top of a double boiler. It will look like black vichyssoise.

When you are ready to serve, and not before, finish the soup by re-heating it in the top of the large double boiler with the drained diced potatoes. Meanwhile, pat the squid dry. Heat the remaining tablespoon of olive oil in a frying pan and toss the squid over high heat. In about a minute, the circles of squid will firm up. Taste one: it should be tender but slightly resistant to the bite. *Do not overcook*. Scrape the squid and its juices into the hot soup and stir.

To serve, fill heated soup plates with soup and garnish with the remaining chopped coriander and julienned pepper strips.

SWORDFISH SOUP

Swordfish is a strong fish that will absorb the flavors of a marinade and then release them into the soup. Be sure not to let the fish sit in the marinade for longer than 30 minutes. After that time, the marinade drains out the juices of the fish, which becomes dry and tasteless.

Marinade:
  8 *cloves, crushed*
  ¼ *cup sweet sherry*
  ¾ *cup white wine*
  2 *tablespoons olive oil*
  3 *tablespoons chopped fresh thyme or 1 teaspoon dried thyme*
  2 *teaspoons coarse salt*
  2 *pounds swordfish, cut ¾-inch thick*

6 *cups Fish Stock I (see page 39)*
2 *small carrots, diced (¾ cup)*
1 *pound Jerusalem artichokes, diced*
1 *medium onion, chopped (1 cup)*
18 *2-inch-long asparagus tips*
Coarse salt and white pepper to taste
1 *tablespoon olive oil*

Combine the cloves, sherry, wine, olive oil, thyme and salt in a small bowl. Cut away the fish skin and bones and cut into serving-size pieces. Put the fish pieces in a flat container and pour the marinade over them. If it doesn't cover the fish completely, you will have to turn the pieces during the marinating period, *which should be no longer than 30 minutes.* Lift out the fish and set it aside, reserving the marinade.

While the fish marinates, heat the stock in a saucepan with the carrots and Jerusalem artichokes. Simmer, covered, for about 30 minutes, or until the vegetables are tender. Remove from the heat.

Pour 4 tablespoons of the marinade into a skillet. Sauté the onion in it, stirring often and adding the marinade little by little until it is all incorporated and the onion is soft and deep golden brown. Scrape it into the stockpot and reheat the stock. When it begins to boil, add the asparagus tips, lower the heat and simmer for a minute or two. Correct the seasoning with salt and pepper to taste.

Pat the fish dry and heat the oil in a skillet large enough to hold the fish without crowding. When the oil is very hot, brown the pieces on both sides. *Do not overcook:* the fish will continue to cook in the hot stock.

To serve, place a piece of fish in each heated bowl and ladle on the piping hot soup and vegetables.

TUNA WITH LEMON GRASS BROTH

Fresh tuna has become readily available since the proliferation of sushi bars. Tuna belly is so highly esteemed for sushi that it is called the caviar of Japan. For this soup, however, you can use the cheaper tuna shank or another firm-textured fish, such as swordfish. Lemon grass, a tropical herb used in South American and Vietnamese cooking, adds a lemony tang; it can be found in Chinese and Spanish markets.

1½ pounds tuna, cut in 2-inch cubes
¼ teaspoon crushed black pepper
2 tablespoons olive oil
6 stalks lemon grass, split halfway down with the base left intact, or ¼ teaspoon lemon grass powder
4 tablespoons butter

4 tablespoons flour
7½ cups Fish Stock I (see page 39), heated
2 teaspoons coarse salt
White pepper
1 cup thinly sliced scallions

Garnish:
½ cup shredded basil leaves

Toss the cubes of tuna with black pepper. In a skillet large enough to hold the fish without crowding, heat the oil. Add the tuna and 2 stalks of the lemon grass and sear the tuna over high heat. Remove the tuna and set it aside, leaving the lemon grass in the pan. (If you are using lemon grass powder, sear the tuna in oil, remove, and then add the powder.) Add the butter to the pan, lower the heat and stir in the flour, cooking it for a minute or so. Then whisk in the hot fish stock and the salt, beating until the broth thickens. Add the remaining lemon grass and stir, scraping up any brown bits of tuna clinging to the bottom of the pan. Let simmer for 5 minutes, then strain through a sieve held over a clean saucepan. Add the white pepper.

To serve, reheat the broth, add the tuna and the scallions and simmer briefly. Then ladle into hot soup plates and garnish with shredded basil.

WOLFFISH AND FIDDLEHEAD SOUP

A truly seasonal soup, one to make in the spring when tiny curled fiddlehead ferns come on the market. Although wolffish is an Atlantic fish, it is less well known here than in Europe, where it is called *lobo* (in Spain) or *loup* (in France.) If you can't find it, substitute another firm, white-fleshed fish, such as tilefish or monkfish or even eel.

2 cloves garlic
1 tablespoon plus 2 teaspoons
   coarse salt
3 tablespoons Anisette
2½ pounds wolffish in one
   piece
5 cups Fish Stock I
   (see page 39)
6 sprigs parsley
1 sprig mint
1 sprig oregano or
   ¼ teaspoon dried oregano

1 bunch celery tops
1-inch piece ginger, pared
¼ teaspoon crushed pepper
¼ teaspoon grated nutmeg
3 tablespoons butter
1 large onion, chopped (2 cups)
½ cup leeks, white part only
1 pound fiddlehead ferns
1 large parsnip, diced (½ cup)

Garnish:
   ½ cup chopped Italian
     parsley

Crush one of the garlic cloves with 1 tablespoon salt and 1 tablespoon Anisette. Rub this mixture into the cavity of the fish and let it sit in the refrigerator at least 2 hours.

In a saucepan, heat 3 cups of the fish stock with a bouquet garni made of the parsley, mint, oregano, celery tops, ginger, pepper and nutmeg tied in cheesecloth. Simmer, partially covered, for 15 minutes. Meanwhile, melt the butter in a second saucepan and sauté the remaining garlic clove, minced, with the onion and leeks, for about 5 minutes or until the onion turns translucent. Stir in the remaining 2 tablespoons of Anisette and cook until it evaporates. Add the fiddleheads and parsnip, tossing them about for a minute before you add the stock and bouquet garni. Bring to a boil, lower the heat and boil gently about 5 minutes.

Place the fish in a large pot with the remaining 2 cups of stock. Ladle the hot stock over the fish, bring back to a boil, reduce the heat and poach the fish in the simmering liquid for 10 to 15 minutes, or until it is fully cooked but still firm. Discard the bouquet garni, add the remaining 2 teaspoons of salt and remove from the heat.

To serve, cut the fish into serving pieces and place in heated soup plates, covered with steaming hot broth and fiddleheads. Sprinkle with chopped parsley.

Meat Soups

Veal Stock

Beef Stock

Aguadito of Ham Hocks and Orzo

Beef and Artichoke Soup

Beef Soup with Kasha

Beef-Mushroom Soup

Beef-Pineapple Soup

Borscht with Braised Beef

Caldo Verde

Flank Steak and Swiss Chard Soup

Lamb with Anchovies Soup

Minestrone with Pesto

Oxtail Soup

Patita

Podacera Soup

Pork and Brown Rice Soup

Pork and Smoked Shrimp Soup

Sweetbread-Shrimp Soup

MEAT STOCKS

Veal and beef stocks require lots of bones and a large stockpot: at least a 10-quart size, and the bigger the better. Both are easy to make but take time and patience for long slow simmering and careful degreasing, so plan to make them when you won't be hurried.

The veal stock is useful for delicate soups; the more full-bodied beef stock is called for in robust soups. Neither has any salt or pepper. That is so that you can season at your own discretion when you use the stocks in soup.

Both can be refrigerated for several days. If you want to extend their lives beyond that, just bring them back to the boil, cool and refrigerate again. If you do this every few days, you can prolong their usefulness until every drop is gone. And, of course, they can be frozen.

VEAL STOCK

7 pounds veal bones
1 veal foot, about 1½ pounds
1 large onion, peeled and
  quartered
1 pound parsnips, pared and
  chopped
6–8 stalks celery, including
  green tops, chopped

2 whole bulbs garlic, cut in half
  horizontally
2-inch piece ginger, pared and
  quartered
1 small bunch fresh dill
3 small bay leaves
8 quarts cold water

Ask the butcher to split the knuckles and the veal foot and cut the bones in 4- to 6-inch lengths. Rinse the bones in cold water. Place them in a large stockpot and add the onion, parsnips, celery, garlic, ginger, dill and bay leaves. Pour in the water. If the pot can't hold all the water, set part of it aside to add later when the liquid has reduced. Bring the contents of the pot to the boil and lower the heat, skimming off any scum that rises to the surface. Simmer, with the surface barely moving, for at least 3 hours; 5 hours is not too long. Keep skimming the surface. Turn off the heat and let the stock cool until the pot is easy to handle. Remove the bones with tongs and let them drain in a colander set over another large pot. Discard the bones and then pour the rest of the stock through the colander. Discard the debris. Remove any fat that rises to the top, or refrigerate the soup overnight and lift off the hardened fat the next day.

BEEF STOCK

8 pounds beef bones
1 whole oxtail, about 2 pounds
1 veal foot, about 1½ pounds
1 pound carrots, chopped
1 pound white turnips, pared and chopped
1 small bunch celery, including green tops, chopped

1 large onion, with the skin left on, quartered
About 9 quarts cold water
12 whole cloves
3 bay leaves
1 small bunch parsley
12 sprigs fresh thyme

Ask the butcher to split the beef knuckles, cut the bones into 4- to 6-inch lengths, cut up the oxtail and split the veal foot. Rinse the bones in cold water and divide between two roasting pans. Put the pans in a 500° oven for 15 minutes. Lower the heat to 450°, turn the bones and roast for another 30 or 40 minutes more, or until the bones are quite brown. Then strew the vegetables over the bones, dividing them between the two pans, and continue to roast, stirring occasionally, until the vegetables take on a rich deep color. This will take another 30 minutes. Do not let the vegetables burn, or the stock will have a bitter flavor.

When the bones and vegetables are a rich brown, transfer them to a stockpot. Drain off the fat from the roasting pans, and put the pans over medium heat and deglaze by pouring in 1 quart of water and stirring the contents until all the brown goodness is combined with the water. Add this liquid to the stockpot and pour in about 8 quarts of water, or as much as the pot will hold. If the pot can't hold all the water, set part of it aside to add later when the liquid has reduced. Add the cloves and bay leaves and bring to a boil, skimming off any scum as it rises to the surface. Lower the heat and simmer, the water barely moving, for at least 3 hours or as long as 5 hours. During the last half hour, add the parsley and thyme. Turn off the heat and let cool until the pot is easy to handle. Then place a colander over another pot. Remove the bones with tongs and put them in the colander to drain. Discard the bones, then pour the rest of the stock through the colander, discarding the debris. There should be 4½ to 5 quarts of stock left. Pour it through a strainer. Skim off any fat that rises to the surface or, if you have time, refrigerate it overnight. In the morning the fat will have hardened and can be lifted off easily.

AGUADITO OF HAM HOCKS AND ORZO

You may know ham hocks as big chunks of meat that are served with sauerkraut. But small ham hocks, weighing around ¾ pound each, are the most delectable, with plenty of luscious gelatinous flesh on them. Ask your butcher for "pigs' knuckles" and he'll give you the right size. Orzo is pasta that looks like rice; it is available in Middle Eastern and other specialty stores.

6–8 fresh ham hocks, about
¾ pound each
Blanching water
1 large onion, unpeeled and
quartered
1 large carrot, coarsely chopped
1 tomato, quartered, or
3 canned plum tomatoes,
cut in half
2 stalks celery, including green
tops, chopped
3 cloves garlic, unpeeled and
crushed
1-inch piece ginger, pared and
cut in half
5 sprigs Italian parsley
5 sprigs cilantro

10 black peppercorns, crushed
2 cloves
1 bay leaf
1 tablespoon plus ½ teaspoon
turmeric
1 cup white wine
¼ cup red wine vinegar
4–5 quarts water
1 tablespoon coarse salt
2 tablespoons olive oil
1 onion, chopped fine (1 cup)
1 cup orzo
Coarse salt and white pepper

Garnish:
⅓–½ cup chopped Italian
parsley leaves

Place the hocks in a large stockpot and cover with cold water. Bring to a boil, lower the heat and blanch for 5 minutes, skimming off the scum that rises to the top. Pour off the blanching water, drain the hocks, clean out the pot and return the hocks to the clean pot.

Add the onion, carrot, tomato, celery, garlic, ginger, parsley, cilantro, peppercorns, cloves, bay leaf, 1 tablespoon of the turmeric, the wine, vinegar and as much of the water as you need to cover the contents of the pot. Add the salt and bring to a boil. Lower the heat and simmer 1½ to 2 hours, adding more water if it is needed to keep the hocks covered. The meat should be very tender but the hocks still intact enough to hold their shape. Remove the pot from the heat, and when it is cool enough to handle, take out the hocks with tongs and set them aside, covering with plastic wrap or a towel to keep them from drying out.

Return the pot to the heat and simmer for another hour, or until the vegetables are very soft and the stock has reduced by a third. Drain through a fine sieve placed over a bowl. Discard the solids and spoon off the fat that rises to the top. There will be about 3 quarts of stock: more than you need for this soup. Keep the extra stock, frozen, to use another time.

To finish the soup, choose a large *sautoir* or deep skillet large enough to hold it all, or use a stockpot along with a small skillet. Heat the oil in the skillet and cook the onion for 5 to 10 minutes, stirring until it is translucent. Stir in the remaining ½ teaspoon of turmeric and cook with the onion for about 1 minute. Add the orzo and the reserved stock and simmer about 10 minutes, when it should be done "al dente." Correct the seasoning with salt and white pepper and remove from the heat.

To serve, place a hock in each soup plate. Ladle on the stock, making sure that each plate contains a good amount of orzo. Sprinkle with chopped parsley. The meat should be tender enough to cut with a soup spoon; you can, however, add a knife and fork to the service if you like.

BEEF AND ARTICHOKE SOUP

A colorful soup that has a heavy perfume of artichokes. Because the meat is briefly sautéed, it remains crisp and tender and never toughens up in the soup pot.

Marinade:
  1 tablespoon chili powder
  1 teaspoon coarse salt
  ½ teaspoon white pepper
  ½ teaspoon cardamom
  2 tablespoons red wine
    vinegar
  1 pound top round, trimmed of
    fat and cut into strips
    ½ by ½ by ¾ inch
  2 tablespoons lemon juice
  4 small artichokes

8 small red onions
2 medium carrots
6 tablespoons olive or
  vegetable oil
4 cloves garlic, peeled
4 tablespoons flour
2½ quarts water
1 large bay leaf
Coarse salt and white pepper

Garnish:
  Chopped fresh Italian parsley

Make a marinade of the chili powder, salt, pepper, cardamom and vinegar. Place the beef strips in a glass bowl and combine the meat and marinade. Set aside at room temperature for 1 hour. Meanwhile, prepare the vegetables. Fill a large basin with water and lemon juice. Break off the artichoke stems and slice off ½ inch of the artichoke top. Using scissors, snip off the leaf tips. Cut the artichokes in quarters, cutting out the furry choke and any small tough leaves near it. As you complete each quarter, drop it in the acidulated water.

Trim and peel the onions, cutting an X in the base of each. Pare and julienne the carrots in 3-inch lengths.

When the meat has marinated for an hour, heat 4 tablespoons of the oil in a large skillet and cook the garlic cloves until they are golden. Add the beef strips, a few at a time, and stir-fry quickly. Using tongs, transfer the browned beef to a plate. Leave the garlic cloves in the pan and stir in the flour, a spoonful at a time, blending with the oil to make a roux. Then add the water, slowly at first, stirring constantly until the mixture is smooth. Add the bay leaf and bring to a boil. Reduce heat and simmer for 15 minutes. Add salt and pepper and then strain through a cheesecloth-lined sieve, squeezing to extract all the garlic juice before you discard the cloth. There should be about 2 quarts of "stock."

In a large casserole with a cover, heat the remaining 2 tablespoons of oil and brown the onions for 5 to 10 minutes. Drain the artichokes and add to the pot with the carrots, tossing to coat with the oil. Pour in the liquid, bring to a boil and simmer for 30 minutes, or until the artichokes are tender but hold their shape. Check the seasoning, put the meat back in the pan and heat briefly.

To serve, place the meat in preheated soup plates with some carrots, onions and artichoke quarters. Ladle in the broth and sprinkle with chopped parsley.

BEEF SOUP WITH KASHA

Make the soup ahead, but don't add the kasha until the last few minutes, giving it just enough time to bloom. If you hold it longer, it will keep absorbing the broth and lose its crisp nutlike taste.

Marinade:
  6 large cloves garlic, minced
  1 tablespoon coarse salt
  1½ teaspoons ground cumin
  1 teaspoon coarsely ground
    pepper
  2 tablespoons balsamic
    vinegar
  2 tablespoons Chinese oyster
    sauce
  2 pounds boneless beef shin,
    cut in 8 equal pieces
  3 tablespoons olive or vegetable
    oil
  2 large onions, chopped
    (3½ cups)

½ teaspoon dried thyme
3 quarts water
1 tablespoon coarse salt
3 stalks celery, diced (1 cup)
3 large carrots, diced (2 cups)
1 cup kasha
1 egg
1 teaspoon sesame oil
White pepper

Garnish:
  ¼ cup chopped Italian
    parsley

To make the marinade, place the garlic and salt in a mortar and mash with a pestle, adding the cumin and pepper to make a smooth paste. Stir in the vinegar and oyster sauce. The mixture will be quite thick. Place the marinade with the meat in a ceramic or glass bowl, toss thoroughly, and set aside at room temperature for 1 hour.

In a large heavy skillet, heat 2 tablespoons of the olive oil and sear the meat in its marinade. Transfer the browned pieces to a plate. Add another tablespoon of olive oil to the same skillet and brown the onions, stirring frequently, for about 10 minutes. When the onions are soft and well browned, spoon them onto a square of cheesecloth, add the thyme leaves, and tie the cloth into a tight bag. Pour the water and salt into the skillet and bring to a boil, skimming off any bits or pieces that rise to the top. Add the meat and the cheesecloth bag and simmer for 45 minutes, skimming the surface frequently. Add the celery and carrots and cook another 45 minutes, or until the meat offers no resistance when pierced with a knife.

While the soup is simmering, place the kasha in a small heavy saucepan. Mix the egg and sesame oil together and stir into the kasha. Cook over very low heat for about 5 minutes, or until the grains become separate and nut-brown. When the grains are very dry, turn off the heat.

When the vegetables and meat are nearly done, remove the cheesecloth bag and let it drain in a strainer over a bowl. Add the kasha to the simmering soup and cook for 10 minutes or until the kasha is just done. When the soup is ready, squeeze the now cooled cheesecloth into the pot and pour in the juices that have drained out of it. Correct the seasoning with white pepper and salt to taste.

To serve, place a piece of meat in each preheated soup plate. Add vegetables and kasha, ladle on the liquid and sprinkle with parsley. Serve with coarse dark bread and sweet butter.

BEEF-MUSHROOM SOUP

A simple but infallible combination. This is a soup to serve not only with a spoon but with a knife and fork and some good strong mustard on the side.

Marinade:
  3 cloves garlic, minced
  2 tablespoons balsamic
    vinegar
  1 tablespoon coarse salt
  1 teaspoon ground cumin
  2 pounds neck beef, in 1¾-inch
    cubes
  6 tablespoons olive or
    vegetable oil
  1 Bermuda onion, peeled,
    layers separated, cut in
    ¾-inch squares

4 tablespoons sweet vermouth
6 tablespoons flour
9 cups Beef Stock (page 74)
1 pound mushrooms
Pepper

Garnish:
  ⅓ cup chopped Italian
    parsley

To make the marinade, combine the garlic, vinegar, salt and cumin and pour it over the beef. Toss so that the meat is completely covered, and set aside to marinate for 1 hour at room temperature.

In a large skillet, heat 2 tablespoons of oil and sauté the pieces of onion for 5 minutes, or until they soften and turn translucent. Add the vermouth and cook until it evaporates. Remove the onion with a slotted spoon, leaving the oil behind in the skillet. The meat will have absorbed nearly all the marinade after an hour. Pat it dry and brush off garlic bits that cling to the cubes. Heat the remaining oil in the skillet and brown the meat on all sides. Do it in two batches if necessary. Remove the meat and add to the reserved onion. Stir the flour into the oil remaining in the skillet, cooking gently until the roux is very brown but not burnt. Then add the stock, cup by cup, stirring constantly so that there are no lumps. Return the meat and onion to the soup and simmer for 1 hour.

Wipe the mushrooms with a damp towel. Leave small mushrooms whole; cut large ones in quarters through the stems. When the soup has cooked for an hour, add the mushrooms and cook for 50 to 60 minutes more, or until the meat is very tender. Correct the seasoning with pepper and salt to taste.

To serve, ladle equal amounts of meat, mushrooms and soup into preheated soup bowls and garnish with chopped parsley.

BEEF-PINEAPPLE SOUP

Although pineapple has a distinct taste, it goes surprisingly well with meat and vegetables. This first-course soup has a rather Polynesian flavor with its thin broth, chunks of meat, peppers and pineapple.

1¼ pounds boneless sirloin tip	*2 large green bell peppers,*
3 tablespoons bacon fat	*cut in 1-inch squares*
1 large Spanish onion,	*6½ cups Beef Stock (page 74)*
cut in 1-inch squares	*2 cups fresh pineapple,*
2 large sweet red peppers,	*cut in 1-inch cubes*
cut in 1-inch squares	*Coarse salt and white pepper*

Trim the beef of all fat and cut it, on the diagonal, into slices ¼ inch thick and 1 inch long.

In a large heavy skillet, heat 2 tablespoons of the bacon fat. Sauté the onion for 5 to 10 minutes, or until lightly browned. Then add the peppers and toss about in the pan just long enough to coat with the oil. Meanwhile, heat the stock to the boiling point in a large stockpot. Scrape in the onion and peppers, add the pineapple and cook for about 4 minutes, or until the peppers are soft. *Do not overcook*: the peppers should retain their bright color. Skim off any scum that rises to the surface. Season with salt and pepper.

Meanwhile, heat the remaining tablespoon of bacon fat in a skillet and sear the strips of meat over high heat, tossing them in the pan to brown them evenly.

To serve, ladle the hot broth with peppers, pineapple and onions into preheated soup plates. Garnish each serving with sautéed beef strips.

BORSCHT WITH BRAISED BEEF

I chose the second cut of brisket for this soup rather than the first cut because it is richer in texture and closer to the look of meat in a Rumanian borscht. Marbled chuck or flanken would also be suitable. Note that the beef is braised without being browned first. It sounds unorthodox, but it works fine.

2–2½ pounds second-cut brisket of beef
Coarse salt and pepper
2–3 large yellow onions, peeled and quartered
2 cloves garlic, peeled (optional)
2 medium beets
1 small head red cabbage
4 stalks celery
1 medium carrot
2 medium potatoes
2–4 cups water

6 cups Beef Stock (page 74)
12 sprigs thyme
12 sprigs parsley
1 bay leaf
2 tablespoons olive oil
2 teaspoons sugar
¾ cup red wine vinegar

Garnish:
½ cup chopped dill
Sour cream mixed with fresh horseradish or Dijon mustard (optional)

Preheat the oven to 325°. Sprinkle the beef with salt and pepper, rubbing the seasoning well into the meat. Place the meat, fat side down, in a heavy pot with a tight-fitting lid. Add 1 onion and the garlic if you like, though the meat will release its juice and become flavorful without any accompaniment. Place the casserole, tightly covered, in the oven and let the meat braise for 1½ hours, turning it over after the first hour of cooking.

While the meat cooks, cut the vegetables into ½-inch dice of uniform size. When the meat has cooked for 1½ hours, test it for tenderness with the tip of a knife—it should meet no resistance. Take the pot out of the oven. If you have used the onion and garlic, strain the juice and discard the vegetables. Put the meat back in the pot, place on top of the stove and add the water and beef stock. Make a bouquet garni by tying together the thyme, parsley and bay leaf in cheesecloth. Bring to a boil, lower the heat and simmer.

In a large frying pan, heat the olive oil and cook the remaining 2 onions cut in ½-inch dice. Cook for 5 minutes. Stir in the beets, cabbage, carrots and celery, sprinkling the vegetables with a little coarse salt and pepper and tossing to coat with the oil. Sprinkle with the sugar and vinegar and continue to cook for 5 to 10 minutes more, or until the vinegar has almost evaporated. Scrape the vegetables, which should still be quite firm, into the simmering stock, rinsing out the frying pan with a little stock and adding it to the soup. Bring the stock back to the boil, reduce the heat, partially cover and simmer for 30 minutes more. The vegetables and stock will have taken on the dominant color of the beets. If the stock has evaporated too much, add some water to the pot. Add the potato cubes and cook for 15 minutes, or until they are thoroughly tender. Season to taste and discard the bouquet garni.

To serve, use a tureen or, if you have used an attractive casserole, bring it right to the table. Cut the beef into savory pieces. Each plate should contain a chunk of meat, a mixture of vegetables and a ladleful of hot stock, all sprinkled with fresh dill. Pass some sour cream mixed with freshly grated horseradish or Dijon mustard so that diners can help themselves. Be sure to put out good black bread and to equip each place with a knife, fork and spoon.

CALDO VERDE

Caldo verde is a familiar dish all over the Iberian Peninsula, but in Portugal it is made in every household. Although recipes differ, the soup usually contains a ham bone or a piece of Spain's remarkable Serrano ham. It always has some of Spain's magnificent olive oil, used in a special way. The olive oil is passed with the soup, and each diner adds as much as he wants, using the oil as a kind of garnish. Obviously, it is important to use the best extra-virgin olive oil you can buy.

½ pound smoked chorizo
  sausages or kielbasa sausage
2 tablespoons olive oil
1 onion, peeled and chopped
  (1 cup)
3 cloves garlic, minced
1 fresh hot pepper, seeded and
  chopped
1 large potato, pared and diced
  (1½ cups)

6–7 cups Veal Stock (page 73)
  or Chicken Stock (page 105)
  or a mixture of the two
½ pound kale
Coarse salt and white pepper

Garnish:
The best olive oil you can buy,
  preferably Spanish

Prick the sausages and blanch them in boiling water for 5 minutes. Drain, cover and set aside.

In a large pot, heat the oil and stir the onion over moderate heat for 5 minutes, or until it begins to soften. Add the garlic and hot pepper and cook for another 5 minutes. Add the diced potato and stock, bring to a boil, lower the heat and simmer for 15 to 20 minutes, or until the potato is nearly fully cooked.

Meanwhile, cut away and discard the tough stems and dull leaves of the kale. Shred the remaining leaves and wash them in several changes of water. Drain and set aside.

When the potato is done, remove 1 cup with a slotted spoon and set it aside to return to the soup later. Purée the rest of the soup in a blender, a few cups at a time. When finished, it should make about 9 cups of very thin broth. Return this to the pot. Slice the chorizos in ½-inch rounds and add them to the broth with the shredded kale. Bring to a boil, reduce the heat and simmer for 10 to 15 minutes, or until the kale softens and loses its bright-green color. The chorizos will still be somewhat chewy. Season to taste with salt and white pepper, return the diced potato and simmer until it is hot.

To serve, ladle the soup into preheated bowls. Each serving should include slices of chorizo, kale, potato and stock. Pass the container of olive oil and show your guests how to pour some oil into each bowl as a seasoning.

FLANK STEAK AND
SWISS CHARD SOUP

Swiss chard is a vegetable that acts as an herb. Not only does it have a strong nutty taste of its own, but when you cook it in broth, it flavors everything around it. In this soup, braised meat, greens and yuca all blend in a broth flavored with Chinese oyster sauce, a thick brown sauce that is made of ground oysters but gives a deep meaty taste.

1 1¼-pound flank steak
2 pounds Swiss chard
¼ cup plus 1 teaspoon olive or
*   vegetable oil*
1 large onion, sliced
1½ teaspoons minced garlic
1 teaspoon ground cumin
Coarse salt
White pepper

3 tablespoons Chinese oyster
*   sauce*
3 quarts Beef Stock (page 74)
1 pound yuca

Garnish:
*   1 bunch scallions with*
*   ½ inch of green, sliced*
*   thin*

Lay the flank steak on your work surface and, using a long sharp knife, cut through the meat horizontally to divide it in half. This is done most easily when the meat is half frozen. You may want to put it in the freezer for 15 minutes before you slice it.

Trim the Swiss chard, rinse and dry. Cut off and reserve the white stems.

In a large skillet, heat 2 tablespoons of oil and sauté the onion over moderate heat for 5 minutes, or until it turns translucent. Stir in the garlic and cumin and cook 1 minute before adding the first handful of Swiss chard. Let each batch of greens wilt before you add the next. When all the green leaves are in the pan, toss them with the onions and garlic, lower the heat and cook until all the water evaporates. When it is completely dry, take the chard out of the pan and put it on a platter. Cool slightly, then pat dry with a paper towel.

Place one of the steaks on your work surface and pound it with a meat pounder or mallet until it widens by at least an inch. Sprinkle with salt and pepper and spread half the chard over the surface of the meat. Starting at the edge nearest you, roll up the meat tightly, enclosing the chard. Tie with butcher's string, starting at the center of the roll and making ties at 1-inch intervals on both sides. The roll should be about 12 inches long. Fix the other steak the same way, and rub oyster sauce on both.

In a large skillet long enough to hold the rolls without bending them, heat 2 more tablespoons of oil and brown the rolls, shaking the pan, so that the meat browns on all sides. Pour in the stock, bring to a boil, reduce the heat and simmer for about 1½ hours, skimming the surface occasionally.

Meanwhile, cut the reserved white stalks of the chard on the diagonal into 3-inch lengths. Pare off the tough yuca bark, cut the yuca in 3-inch lengths, cover with salted water and boil for 20 minutes, or until tender. Drain and separate into segments.

About 30 minutes before the meat is done, heat 1 teaspoon of oil in a frying pan and toss the stalks of chard over medium heat for about 10 minutes, or until they are golden in color but still crunchy.

When the meat is tender, take it out of the stock and let cool slightly. Pour the stock through a fine sieve and return to the pot. Add the stalks of chard and cook for about 5 minutes more, or until barely tender. Then add the yuca to heat through. Correct the seasoning.

Cut the strings from the meat and slice each roll on the diagonal into 2½-inch slices.

To serve, divide the meat among heated soup bowls with the chard stalks and yuca. Ladle in hot broth and sprinkle each bowl with sliced scallions.

LAMB WITH ANCHOVIES SOUP

This is another example of the affinity that meat and fish have for each other. It is an unusual combination, but the pungency and bite of the anchovies help to bring out the luscious taste of the lamb. Italian cooks prefer salt-cured anchovies, but you can use ordinary canned anchovies in oil for the marinade.

Marinade:
  1 tablespoon coarse salt
  3 cloves garlic, chopped
  1 teaspoon dried spearmint
    leaves
  ½ teaspoon ground cumin
  ¼ teaspoon cayenne pepper
  ⅛ teaspoon ground cloves
  1 2-ounce can anchovy filets,
    drained
  2 tablespoons wine vinegar
  1 tablespoon soy sauce
  1 tablespoon olive oil
  1 teaspoon sesame oil
2–2½ pounds breast, neck or
  shoulder of lamb in
  2-inch squares (there should
  be 12–16 pieces)

2–3 tablespoons olive or
  vegetable oil
2 tablespoons flour
3 quarts water
1 bay leaf
2 tablespoons cornstarch,
  dissolved in ¼ cup water
Coarse salt and white pepper
1½ pounds potatoes, pared and
  diced
1½ pounds celery root, pared
  and diced
1 cup tightly packed cilantro, or
  ¾ cup Italian parsley with
  ¼ cup mint

To make the marinade, put the salt and garlic in a mortar and mash with a pestle to make a paste. (If you don't have a mortar and pestle, you can use a blender or mash by hand.) Mash in the spearmint, cumin, cayenne pepper and cloves. Chop the drained anchovies and mash them into the mixture with the pestle. Stir in the vinegar, soy sauce and two oils.

Toss the lamb with the marinade in a glass or ceramic bowl. Set aside to marinate for 8 hours at room temperature or overnight in the refrigerator.

In a large skillet, heat 2 tablespoons of the oil and brown the marinade-coated pieces of lamb. Some of the marinade is sure to stick to the bottom of the pan in brown bits. Don't worry about it. Scrape the meat into a stockpot. Stir any marinade left in the bowl into the skillet, add the flour and blend well. Add 1 quart of the water, stirring constantly so that there are no lumps and the liquid thickens slightly. Pour this liquid through a strainer into the stockpot with the remaining 2 quarts of water and a bay leaf. Bring to a boil, lower the heat and simmer for 1 hour, or until the meat is just barely tender. It will cook again with the vegetables, so don't let it get too soft at this point.

With a slotted spoon, remove the meat and set it aside. Remove and discard the bay leaf. Skim the stock, removing all the fat. Pour the cornstarch-water mixture into the fat-free stock, stirring as the liquid thickens. Correct the seasoning with salt and white pepper to taste. Add the potatoes, celery root and cooked lamb to the pot. Bring to a boil, lower the heat and simmer for 20 to 30 minutes more, or until the meat and vegetables are completely tender. When the soup is done, add the chopped cilantro or parsley and mint and cook for 2 minutes.

To serve, place 2 pieces of meat with equal amounts of potato and celery root into thoroughly preheated plates (an essential with lamb). Ladle on the herbed soup and serve at once.

MINESTRONE WITH PESTO

A nearly classic minestrone, except for the hominy in the soup and the ginger in the pesto. Make it with water or with beef stock—if you use the stock, you won't have to make the bouquet garni.

Pesto:
  2 cups tightly packed basil
    leaves, stems removed and
    reserved
  4–5 tablespoons olive oil
  1 teaspoon minced garlic
  1 teaspoon chopped ginger
  2 teaspoons coarse salt
1 leek, white part with 1 inch
  of green, chopped
2 fresh hot chile peppers or
  12 black peppercorns,
  crushed
1 bay leaf
½ teaspoon dried oregano
2 cloves
1–2 tablespoons olive oil

1 large onion, diced
2 carrots, diced
2 stalks celery, diced
½ pound celery root, diced
  (1 cup)
2 quarts water or Beef Stock
  (page 74)
1 cup cooked hominy
  (canned white corn kernels)
1 cup cooked or canned
  chick-peas, drained
Coarse salt and white pepper

Garnish:
  ½ cup freshly grated
    Parmesan cheese

First make the pesto. Chop the basil leaves and place in a blender or food processor with 4 tablespoons of the olive oil, the garlic, ginger and salt. Process until you have a thoroughly integrated, smooth, thick mixture. Add another tablespoon of oil if necessary. Scrape the pesto into a measuring cup: you should have ½ cup. Cover and refrigerate.

Make a bouquet garni, putting the leek, reserved basil stems, hot peppers or peppercorns, bay leaf, oregano and cloves on an 8-inch square of cheesecloth and tying it securely.

In a large skillet or saucepan, heat the olive oil and stir the onion over moderate heat for about 5 minutes, or until it is translucent. Add the carrots, celery, celery root and sauté all the vegetables together for 2 to 3 minutes. Pour in the water and bouquet garni, or the beef stock without a bouquet garni. Bring to a boil, reduce heat and simmer, partially covered, for about 30 minutes, or until the vegetables are tender.

Remove the bouquet garni, first squeezing it over the pot to extract all its goodness. Add the drained hominy and chick-peas to the soup and cook only long enough to heat through. Stir in half the pesto and correct the seasoning with salt and pepper.

To serve, ladle the soup into heated plates and drop dollops of the remaining ¼ cup of pesto in small mounds in the center of each serving. Sprinkle with Parmesan cheese and serve with crusty Italian bread.

OXTAIL SOUP

I have a passion for the meaty taste of oxtails. Thick substantial oxtail soups are more popular in Europe than they are here. I've done a simple version of the rich peasant soup, one that exploits the deep, full taste of the meat.

2 oxtails, 2–2½ pounds each,
   cut into 2-inch pieces
Marinade:
   ½ cup olive oil
   ½ cup balsamic vinegar
   6 large cloves garlic, minced
   2 teaspoons coarse salt
   2 teaspoons ground black
     pepper
4 quarts water
1 pound carrots, chopped
4 stalks celery, with green tops,
   chopped
1 large onion, peeled and
   quartered
2-inch piece ginger, pared and
   cut in half

6 whole cloves
2 bay leaves
1 cup red wine
2 tablespoons olive oil
1 cup minced onions
1 cup crushed canned Italian
   plum tomatoes
5 tablespoons flour
3–4 teaspoons coarse salt
6 medium carrots, cubed
8 potatoes, cubed

Garnish:
  ⅓–½ cup chopped Italian
    parsley

Put the oxtails in a large glass or ceramic dish and toss with a marinade made by mixing the olive oil, vinegar, garlic, salt and pepper. Let stand for 30 minutes at room temperature.

Pour some of the marinade into a large skillet and brown the meat thoroughly on all sides, adding additional marinade as you need it. Transfer the meat to a stockpot and deglaze the skillet with 1 quart of the water, stirring to incorporate all the brown goodness. Pour this into the stockpot with the carrots, celery, onion, ginger, cloves, bay leaves, the remaining 3 quarts of water and the wine. The liquid should cover the meat by at least 2 inches. Bring to a boil, reduce heat and simmer for about 3 hours, skimming off any scum that rises to the surface.

When the meat almost falls off the bone, remove the pot from the heat. When cool enough to handle, remove the oxtail pieces to a platter with tongs. Pour the liquid through a colander set over a saucepan and discard the solids. Strain the liquid. There should be about 2½ cups of stock. If there is more, cook down until the stock is reduced to that amount.

In a large skillet, heat the olive oil and add the minced onions, stirring over moderate heat for about 5 minutes, or until the onions become translucent. Add the tomatoes and cook for 5 minutes, or until the mixture thickens. Stir in the flour and combine thoroughly. Add the reserved stock to the tomato mass, a cup at a time, stirring contantly, as the soup thickens. Add 3 teaspoons of salt, the cubed carrots and potatoes and simmer until the vegetables are tender, continuing to skim off the scum that rises. Just before the vegetables are ready, return the oxtails to the soup to reheat. Correct the seasoning.

To serve, put the oxtails on a platter, surround them with the vegetables and moisten all with a little stock. Garnish with parsley. Then, at the table, divide the oxtails among the heated plates so that each serving has its share of large and small pieces, plus carrots and potatoes. Ladle hot stock over the meat and serve with a good crusty bread.

PATITA

A patita is a veal foot boned and filled with savory stuffing. The foot will be around a foot long. If you have a large *sautoir*, you can lay the veal foot in it and add only enough water—about 4 quarts—to cover the meat and vegetables. If you have to use a tall stockpot, the veal foot will stand on end, more water will be needed, and you'll end up with a bonus of leftover stock to reduce or to freeze as it is. This recipe is worth the trouble—especially on a rainy day.

2 veal feet, 1¾–2 pounds each
2 carrots, chopped
3 stalks celery, including leaves, chopped
1 onion, peeled and quartered
1 whole bulb garlic, cut in half horizontally
1 bunch Italian parsley
3 dried hot red peppers
2 bay leaves
8 juniper berries
2 tablespoons coarse salt
8 quarts cold water

Mushroom stuffing:
1 ounce dried morels
1 cup warm water

½ pound white mushrooms
1–2 tablespoons olive oil or vegetable oil
½ cup minced onion
2 tablespoons sherry
1 egg
2 teaspoons coarse salt
½ cup fresh breadcrumbs
1–1½ tablespoons wine vinegar

Garnish:
⅓ cup chopped Italian parsley

Singe the veal feet over a flame and rinse them in cold water. Place the feet, carrots, celery, onion, garlic, parsley, chile peppers, bay leaves and juniper berries in a stockpot. Add the salt and as much of the water as you need to cover the contents of the pot. Bring to a boil. Lower the heat and simmer for 2½ hours, adding more water from time to time if necessary to keep the contents covered. At the end of this time, the meat should be falling away from the bones.

While the soup is simmering, make the mushroom stuffing. Soak the morels in warm water for 1 hour, or until they are soft. Then cut them in half with scissors, rinse them to get rid of the sand, drain and pat dry. Wipe the white mushrooms with a damp cloth and chop fine. Chop the drained morels. Heat the oil in a heavy pan and cook the onion for a few minutes until it softens. Add the chopped mushrooms, morels and sherry. Stir frequntly over low heat until the mushrooms have released all their liquid. Cook and stir for at least 20 minutes, or until the liquid evaporates and the mushroom bits are dry. Transfer these "duxelles" to a bowl to cool. Then beat the egg and salt together and stir into the duxelles with the bread crumbs. Set aside.

When the veal feet are cooked, remove the pot from the stove and let the stock cool. When you can remove the feet, do so, handling them carefully to keep them intact.

Cut 2 sheets of foil, 12 by 16 inches, and lay them down with the long side next to you. Wipe the cooked feet and place each one in the center of a sheet of foil, so that its length is parallel to the length of the foil. Do this while the feet are warm; if they are allowed to cool, they will firm up more than you want.

Remove the bones one at a time, including the small bones concealed in the center of the feet. Discard them, and flatten the surface facing you. It will be an uneven mass of meat, gelatinous gristle and tendons. Remove the gristle and tendons.

Divide the stuffing in half and spread half over each foot, smoothing the mixture with your hands to cover most of the surface but leaving an inch clear around the edges. Wash and dry your hands and wipe away any stuffing that has fallen onto the foil.

Starting with the side closest to you, use the foil to fold the skin over the filling until you reach the center. Then fold the skin farthest away toward the center. With the aid of the foil, roll the enclosed filling and skin as tightly as possible, until the foil encloses the whole roll. Twist the ends. The roll will now look like a fat party favor 7 inches long and 1½ to 2 inches thick. Push the twisted ends into the roll to press out the air. Repeat with the second roll. Tear off two more 12- by 16-inch sheets of foil and wrap each roll in a second sheet, using the same twists. Insulate the contents completely and set the rolls aside.

Drain the stock through a colander and then through a cheesecloth-lined sieve or strainer. Return the broth to the cleaned stockpot, bring to a boil and drop in the two foil-covered rolls. Turn off the heat, cover and let them sit there for 10 minutes. Then lift out the rolls, wipe them dry and refrigerate them overnight.

Taste the broth. It should be light and flavorful enough, but you may want to reduce it further by simmering for an hour. Correct the seasoning and refrigerate the broth overnight.

An hour or so before serving time, remove the rolls from the refrigerator and unwrap the foil. Cut off and discard the ends of each roll, and cut each one into 8 slices ¾ inch thick. Cover them and let them come to room temperature. It will take 45 minutes. Remove the broth from the refrigerator, skim off the fat and pour 2 quarts into a saucepan. Bring to a boil, skimming off any foam that rises to the surface. Correct the seasoning once again and stir in the sherry wine vinegar to give the broth a slight sharpness.

To serve, place two slices of patita in each preheated soup plate. Ladle on the hot broth and sprinkle with parsley.

PODACERA SOUP

Although we usually see mustard seeds in the form of powder mixed with vinegar, there is an old tradition of using them whole in meat dishes. Black mustard seeds—the best kind—are here used whole in succulent pork dumplings.

1½ pounds pork shoulder, rump or fresh ham, ground twice
1 onion, minced (1 cup)
1 teaspoon minced garlic
1½ tablespoons each finely diced green, yellow and red bell peppers
1 cup fresh white bread crumbs
1 tablespoon coarse salt
¼ teaspoon mace
¼ teaspoon cinnamon

10 pitted prunes, diced (a heaping ¼ cup)
1 tablespoon black mustard seeds
1 1¼-pound celery root
9 cups fat-free Chicken Stock (page 105)
Coarse salt and white pepper

Garnish:
⅓–½ cup chopped Italian parsley or cilantro

Combine the pork, onion, garlic, diced peppers, bread crumbs, salt, mace and cinnamon in a large bowl. Add the prunes, using your hands to see that they don't clump together but are dispersed through the mixture. In a cast-iron skillet, toast the mustard seeds over moderate heat, shaking the pan constantly. When the seeds begin to darken and jump about and give off a distinct aroma, they are done. Sprinkle them over the meat mixture, stir to combine and refrigerate the mixture in a covered bowl; the chilling will firm it up and help the dumplings hold their shape.

Pare the celery root and cut enough into ½-inch dice to make 2 cups. Cover with cold water and set aside.

Heat the chicken stock in a large pot while you make the dumplings. Place a sheet of waxed paper on your surface and form oval-shaped dumplings, each a generous ounce, with your hands. When they are finished, there should be between 24 and 30 dumplings.

Drop the dumplings into the simmering stock one at a time. When all are in the pot, lower the heat and let them poach for 5 minutes, or until they rise to the top. Cook a few minutes more. Remove one of the dumplings and cut it in half to see if it is cooked: there should be no hint of red in the center. Using a slotted spoon, carefully transfer the dumplings to a platter in a single layer and cover lightly to keep warm.

Strain the stock through a cheesecloth-lined sieve. Rinse out the pan, return the stock and bring it back to the boiling point. Add the drained celery root and simmer for 10 minutes. Taste for seasoning, adding salt and white pepper to your liking. Return the dumplings to the broth to reheat and remove the pan from the stove.

To serve, ladle the piping hot soup into preheated soup plates with equal amounts of dumplings and celery root in each serving. Sprinkle with chopped herbs.

PORK AND BROWN RICE SOUP

A glutinous juicy porridge flavored with the licorice taste of fennel. The secret of the meat's crisp rind is letting it dry out thoroughly. How long will that take? All I can say is that when you think it's absolutely dry, you should give it another hour.

2½–3 pounds fresh pork belly
or a thick slab of fresh bacon
1 tablespoon cracked pepper
2 pounds onions
4 bulbs fennel with green
feathery tops
½ teaspoon dried rosemary
8–12 black peppercorns,
crushed
8–12 whole allspice, crushed
1½ pounds pork bones or
the base of fresh spareribs,
cut in 1–2-inch pieces
1 12-ounce bottle beer
2½ quarts water
2 teaspoons coarse salt

Filling for pork:
1 clove garlic, chopped
2 teaspoons coarse salt
1½ teaspoons ground cumin
½ teaspoon cinnamon
⅛ teaspoon ground cloves
3 teaspoons green
peppercorns, drained
2 tablespoons butter
⅓ cup fresh bread crumbs
1–2 tablespoons olive or
vegetable oil
1 cup brown rice
Coarse salt and pepper to taste

With a sharp knife, score the pork rind into diamonds by slashing on the diagonal. Then dry the meat with paper towels and rub with cracked pepper. Place on a rack, rind side up and let sit for several hours at room temperature. If possible, place it close to the heat or a fan. After a few hours the rind should be thoroughly dry and appear papery.

When the skin is dry, preheat the oven to 400° while you prepare the vegetables. Cut away the root ends of the onions, but leave the skins on. Cut in thick slices. Cut off the tops of the fennel, removing enough of the smallest feathery green tops to make 1 cup, tightly packed. Then chop the stalks and 2 of the bulbs and add to the onions. Reserve the remaining 2 bulbs to quarter and cook in the soup later. Toss the onions and fennel with the rosemary, peppercorns and allspice. Place in a mound in the center of a large heavy roaster, with the pork bones around it. Put a rack on top of the vegetables and set the pork on it, rind side up. Put the pan in the center of the oven and roast for 1 hour, or until the rind is fairly crisp and the pork nearly cooked. Take the meat and rack from the mound and set aside to cool.

Stir the now softened vegetables with the bones and let them roast 20 to 30 minutes more, or until the vegetables are browned. Remove from the oven and, using a slotted spoon, transfer the vegetables and bones to a stockpot. Pour away the fat and deglaze the roasting pan with the beer, stirring over moderate heat to get up the brown bits at the bottom of the pan. Place the beer mixture into the stockpot with the water and salt and bring to a boil. Lower the heat and simmer, partially covered, for 45 minutes to 1 hour. Then pour through a fine strainer set over a container. Discard the bones and press the vegetables to get all the goodness from them before discarding them. Degrease the liquid and return to the stockpot, adding enough water to make 2 quarts.

Turn the oven down to 350° and make the filling for the pork. Place the garlic, salt, cumin, cinnamon and cloves in a mortar. Mash with the pestle until the garlic disappears. Then mash in the green peppercorns and butter, and when the mixture is totally smooth, stir in the bread crumbs.

Using a long sharp knife, cut the slab of pork horizontally so that the top with the rind is thinner than the bottom piece. Lift off the top in one piece and spread the filling over the lower part. Carefully replace the top and press the pieces together. Place on a rack set in a roasting pan and return to the oven to roast for at least 30 minutes.

While the pork is roasting, finish the soup. Quarter the 2 reserved fennel bulbs. Heat 1 tablespoon of the oil in a skillet and sauté the fennel, tossing, for about 5 minutes, or until it is golden. Remove and set aside. Add more oil to the pan and brown the rice, then transfer it to the pot of stock. Bring the rice and stock to a boil, lower the heat and simmer for 25 minutes, skimming frequently. Add the fennel and simmer another 25 minutes, or until the fennel is tender, the rice cooked and the stock is like a thin porridge. Correct the seasoning with salt and pepper, but remember that the roast pork is highly seasoned.

Check the pork: it should be done, with a crisp rind. It can remain in the oven, with the heat turned off, until the soup is ready.

To serve, cut the meat into diamond-shaped pieces. Fill the preheated soup plates with the porridgy soup. Place a piece of fennel and a piece of meat, crisp side up, in each bowl. Sprinkle with the feathery green fennel leaves and serve with a knife, fork and soup spoon.

PORK AND SMOKED SHRIMP SOUP

This is such a simple soup to make that the hardest part will be persuading the butcher to sell you so little pork butt. If he won't do it, buy a thick center-cut pork chop, bone it and render the fat to use for browning. Or plan ahead by cutting half a pound of meat from a pork roast and freezing it until you're ready to make the soup. Smoked shrimp is becoming reasonably available, but if you can't find any, fresh shrimp is a suitable substitute.

½ pound fresh pork butt
2 tablespoons rendered pork or
*   bacon fat*
3½ quarts water
2 teaspoons coarse salt
1 small green cabbage, about
*   2 pounds*
1 large green apple

¾ pound smoked or fresh
*   shrimp*
Pepper to taste

Garnish:
*   ⅓ cup snipped dill or*
*   chopped Italian parsley*

Cut the pork into slices ½ inch thick, and cut the slices into 1-inch squares. Set aside. Heat the pork fat and brown the pork in it. Transfer the pork to a stockpot. Add 3 quarts of the water and the salt, bring to a boil, reduce heat and simmer for 45 minutes, or until the meat is very tender.

While the meat cooks, prepare the rest of the ingredients. Cut the cabbage in 8 wedges, first cutting away any discolored outside leaves. Trim the core at the base, but leave enough intact to hold the wedges together. Rinse in cold water, drain and set aside. Pare and core the apple and cut into 8 wedges. Place in cold water to keep from discoloring. If you have smoked shrimp, remove the shells and legs, leaving on the tail; if you have fresh shrimp, also remove the vein that runs down the back.

When the pork is tender, add the cabbage to the pot. As the cabbage cooks and becomes reduced in volume, press it down gently so that it is covered with liquid. Add the remaining water and simmer for 10 to 15 minutes, or until the cabbage is barely tender but still green. Then place the apple wedges on top of the cabbage. If you're using fresh shrimp, add them at this time, pushing them down into the liquid. When they have simmered for 3 to 4 minutes, they will turn pink. By then the apples should be soft and the cabbage quite tender. If you're using smoked shrimp, which need only be heated for a minute, wait until you are nearly ready to eat before you add them to the pot. Add the pepper and correct the seasoning. (You may need more salt if you are using fresh shrimp.)

To serve, place a wedge of cabbage, a piece of apple, 1 or 2 shrimp and several pieces of pork in each soup plate. Ladle the stock over it all and garnish with chopped dill or parsley.

SWEETBREAD-SHRIMP SOUP

Search for shrimp with heads and tails on to use as the base of the shrimp stock. If you have shrimp shells saved in the freezer, add them to the stock: don't be afraid to use too many shells. If you can get only shrimp with the heads and tails removed, replace the water in the recipe with Fish Stock I (page 39), Chicken Stock (page 105) or Vegetable Stock (page 3) or even with diluted clam juice.

2 pounds veal sweetbreads
16 large shrimp (1½ pounds)
  with heads and tails intact
2 medium carrots, chopped
2 parsnips, chopped
4 stalks celery, with green tops,
  chopped
1 large onion, peeled and
  quartered
2 2-inch pieces ginger, pared
  and cut in half
12 sprigs fresh tarragon or dill
  or 1 tablespoon dried
  tarragon or dill

6 juniper berries
2 bay leaves
2 quarts water (see note above)
½ cup plus 2 tablespoons butter
8 tablespoons flour, plus flour
  for dredging
3 cups milk
Coarse salt and white pepper

Garnish:
  3-4 teaspoons chopped
    tarragon, parsley or dill

You can do some of the preparation of the sweetbreads a day ahead. Cover them with cold water and refrigerate for 3 to 4 hours, changing the water once or twice, or let them sit in the refrigerator overnight. If you are in a hurry, you can place the sweetbreads in the sink and let cold tap water run into the bowl for at least 30 minutes, or until the water is clear. When you are ready to cook the sweetbreads, drain and place in a saucepan covered with cold water. Bring just to the point of boiling: never let sweetbreads come to a rolling boil. Lower the heat and simmer—the water should barely move—for 15 minutes. Remove from the stove, drain out the water and chill the sweetbreads under cold running water or by filling the pan with ice water. When they are cool, pull away any fat, sinew, tough membranes or dark spots that you see. It's all right if some lobes of the meat separate from the rest.

Pressing the sweetbreads can make the difference between meat that is tender and meat that is rubbery. Line a baking sheet with a kitchen towel, letting half fall loose over the edge. Put the drained sweetbreads on the towel, and fold the loose half over them. Put a plate or a second baking sheet over the towel and weigh it down with a few heavy objects, such as large cans of tomatoes, pots filled with water, heavy crocks. Leave for at least 2 hours or, even better, overnight in the refrigerator.

Now prepare the shrimp and stock. If you have found whole shrimp, remove the heads and tails, shell the shrimp and refrigerate. Put the shells, heads and tails in a large saucepan with the carrots, parsnips, celery, onion, ginger, fresh tarragon, juniper berries and bay leaves. Cover with water and bring to a boil. Lower the heat and simmer, skimming the surface now and then, for at least 30 minutes. Pour through a colander over a large pot, and discard the debris. There should be at least 2 quarts of liquid, which should be poured through a medium strainer and reserved.

In a large saucepan, heat ½ cup of the butter until it melts. Then stir in 8 tablespoons of flour over low heat and cook the two together for 3 minutes. Remove from the heat and add the milk, stirring constantly. Return the pan to the stove and cook. Stir this béchamel sauce until it becomes quite thick.

Heat the reserved shrimp stock or substitute stock. Whisk into the béchamel until the two are combined in a smooth, silky soup with the consistency of a thin vichyssoise. Season with salt and white pepper and keep warm over low heat while you prepare the sweetbreads and shrimp.

Cut the pressed sweetbreads into 16 pieces. Flour lightly and sprinkle with salt and pepper. Heat the remaining 2 tablespoons of butter in a large skillet and brown the sweetbreads on both sides. If there's room in the pan, stir in the reserved shrimp and toss them, too, in the butter for 2 to 3 minutes, or until they turn pink but are still slightly under-cooked. (If you have to use another pan because the skillet isn't large enough, add 1 tablespoon butter to the pan before adding the shrimp.) Scrape the shrimp and pieces of sweetbread into the soup, turn up the heat and return to a simmer.

To serve, place two sweetbread pieces and two shrimp in each pre-heated soup plate. Ladle in the creamy white soup and garnish with chopped fresh herbs.

Poultry and Game Soups

CHICKEN STOCK

You should always have homemade chicken stock in your freezer. When you cook a chicken, put the backs, necks and wing tips in a plastic bag in the freezer until you have collected enough and have the time to make stock. If you're lucky enough to have a butcher who gets whole chickens (most of them don't), you should ask him to give you the feet for your stockpot. Before you use them, singe them over an open flame and wipe them with a cloth to take off the skin.

4½–5 pounds chicken backs, wings, necks, gizzards and feet
2 stalks celery, chopped, including leaves
2 medium carrots, pared and chopped (1½ cups)
2 medium onions, cut in half, skins left on

6–8 sprigs fresh thyme or ½ teaspoon dried thyme
6–8 sprigs fresh dill
6–8 sprigs fresh parsley
⅛ teaspoon black peppercorns
2–3 whole cloves

Rinse the chicken parts, pulling off obvious clumps of fat. Put in a 6- to 8-quart stockpot with the remaining ingredients. Bring to a boil, skimming off the scum that rises to the top. Lower the heat and simmer for at least 2 hours. If you keep the stock at a gentle simmer, never letting it boil hard, it will be quite clear. When it is done, let it cool. Strain and skim off any fat that rises to the surface. Or you can pour the stock into a large bowl or pot, refrigerate overnight, and then lift off the hardened fat with a spoon. Please note that the stock is not salted so that it can be used in other recipes.

CLARIFIED CHICKEN STOCK

Clarifying the stock will produce a beautiful amber broth, with enhanced flavor and richness. Add garnishes such as sliced scallions, julienned carrots, celery or thinly sliced mushrooms and you have a consommé suitable for any occasion.

¾ pound chicken, ground
1 cup diced celery
1 cup diced carrots
12 sprigs thyme

5 eggs
2½ quarts fat-free Chicken
Stock (see preceding page),
cold

Combine the ground chicken, celery, carrots and thyme. Separate the eggs, reserving the yolks and adding the whites *and crushed shells* to the chicken mixture. Place in a stockpot and stir in the cold, fat-free chicken stock. Bring to a boil over low heat, stirring constantly. The whites will start to foam and come to the top. Immediately stop stirring. Reduce heat and let the stock simmer for 15 minutes. Do not stir the stock during this time, so that the whites and other ingredients can come together and form a crust at the top of the pot. After 15 minutes, check for clarity by separating a small part of the crust. The liquid below should be very clear. If it is not, simmer for 5 minutes more and check again. Turn off the heat and let the soup cool slightly.

Line a colander with several layers of cheesecloth and put it over a container. Tilting the pot, pour the stock gently into the colander, holding back the crust as best you can. When all the stock has been strained, let the crust drain for a few minutes. You should have a little more than 2 quarts of clear amber stock.

AGUADITO OF DUCK

Aguadito? It's a South American tradition, a porridgy soup thickened with rice and flavored, always, with cilantro. There is usually some chicken or game as well, as in this version, where duck adds its richness to the porridge.

1 4½- to 5-pound duck
2 carrots, chopped (1½ cups)
3 stalks celery, chopped
  (¾ cup)
1 inch ginger, pared and cut in
  half lengthwise
4 cloves garlic
1 large onion, peeled and
  quartered
3 quarts plus 1 cup water
1 12-ounce bottle beer

1 large onion, chopped
2 teaspoons minced garlic
2 fresh hot green chile peppers,
  seeded and minced
1 cup long-grain rice
2 teaspoons coarse salt
White pepper

Garnish:
  ½ cup chopped coriander

Have the butcher bone the duck. Cut each half of the breast into two pieces on the diagonal and cut the thigh and leg apart: 8 serving pieces in all. Set aside while you prepare the duck stock from the rest of the bird.

Place the duck carcass, neck, gizzards (but not the liver) and scraps in a roasting pan. Surround with the chopped carrots, celery, ginger, garlic cloves and quartered onion and roast for 30 minutes in a 450° oven, stirring now and then, until bones and vegetables are a deep golden brown. Remove from the pan with a slotted spoon and place in a stockpot. Pour off the fat from the roasting pan and deglaze by pouring in 1 cup of water and stirring until all the brown goodness is incorporated. Pour the deglazing liquid into the stockpot with the beer and the remaining 3 quarts of water. Bring to a boil, turn down the heat and simmer for 1 hour, skimming off any scum that rises to the top. Strain through a napkin-lined colander, discard the debris and set aside. There should be at least 2 quarts of stock.

In a large pan, heat 1 tablespoon of duck fat. When it is melted, add the chopped onion and cook for 5 minutes, or until it turns translucent. Stir in the garlic and hot pepper and cook for another minute. Add the raw rice and stir to cover with fat. Add the duck stock and salt and bring to a simmer. Cover the pot and cook for about 20 minutes.

When the rice is half done, score the duck skin in a diamond pattern. Dry it well and place the duck pieces, skin side down, in a hot skillet with 1 tablespoon of duck fat. When the skin is well browned, turn the duck and cook briefly on the flesh side. The finished duck should have crisp skin and a pink interior. Keep warm while you finish the soup, which will now be thick and porridgy. Correct the seasoning with pepper and salt to taste.

To serve, ladle a generous amount of the soupy rice into each bowl with a piece of duck and some chopped coriander. Serve with a knife, fork and spoon.

BITTER ALMOND AND MATZOH BALL SOUP

The taste of bitter almonds is familiar through Italian almond cookies, but the nuts themselves are just about impossible to find because generally they are processed into oils, which go into flavorings. Apricot kernels make a respectable substitute, and can be found in Chinese or Hungarian groceries. The third-best choice is hazelnuts. This soup is a big break with tradition, for the familiar matzoh balls have an unexpected crunch and bitter-sweet flavor that lends them excitement.

6 tablespoons plus 1 teaspoon
vegetable oil
1½ ounces bitter almonds,
apricot kernels or hazelnuts
1½ cups matzoh meal
6 tablespoons ground almonds
(a scant ½ cup before
grinding)
2 tablespoons plus 2 teaspoons
coarse salt

6 eggs
¾ cup club soda
6 quarts water
2 quarts Chicken Stock
(page 105)

Garnish:
½ cup chopped dill

In a skillet, heat 1 teaspoon of the oil and toast the bitter almonds or apricot kernels over moderate heat, shaking the pan, until they turn a dark brown. Remove from the pan and chop coarsely. Place them in a bowl, along with the matzoh meal, ground almonds and 2 teaspoons of the salt. Beat the eggs and the rest of the oil together and stir into the matzoh mixture. Pour in the club soda, cover the bowl and refrigerate for 1 hour.

In a large wide-mouth pot, bring the water to a boil with the rest of the salt. Form matzoh balls by rolling them in your palms, dipping your hands into ice water now and then to prevent sticking. You should have about 18 balls, each 1½ to 2 inches in diameter. When the water boils, reduce heat and drop in the balls one by one. Cover the pot and let simmer for 30 minutes, or until they are firm in the center. Test by cutting one in half and tasting it.

While the matzoh balls are cooking, heat the chicken stock in another large pot. Transfer the matzoh balls to the pot of chicken stock and let them simmer for about 5 minutes. Correct the seasoning.

To serve, place 2 matzoh balls in each heated soup bowl and fill with steaming chicken soup. Sprinkle with dill.

CABBAGE ROLL SOUP

Most cabbage soups are rough, hearty fare. This one is more delicate, a well-flavored broth in which little packages of stuffed cabbage simmer.

1 pound skinned and boned
  chicken breast
½ pound ground pork
¼ teaspoon saffron
¼ cup dry sherry
½ cup raisins
1 head green cabbage,
  3½–4 pounds
2 tablespoons vegetable oil
1 cup chopped onion

1 tablespoon minced garlic
¾ cup soft fresh bread crumbs
4 teaspoons coarse salt
¼ teaspoon white pepper
½ cup pignoli nuts
2½ quarts Chicken Stock
  (page 105)

Garnish:
  Fresh dill leaves

Grind the chicken in a grinder or chop very fine with a knife. Using your hands, combine with the pork and refrigerate.

Fill a stockpot with water and bring to a boil on top of the stove. Meanwhile, soak the saffron in 1 tablespoon of the sherry for at least 15 minutes. Place the raisins in another bowl with the remaining sherry and let soak.

Remove discolored leaves from the cabbage and cut out and discard the core. When the water boils, drop the cabbage into the pot and boil for 10 to 15 minutes. Remove it from the pot and drop it into a large basin of ice water. Peel off as many soft leaves as you can, setting them aside to drain. Return the cabbage to the boiling water and let it cook until you can remove more tender leaves. Continue until you have 16 softened cabbage leaves.

In a small skillet, heat the oil and sauté the onion for 5 minutes, or until it is translucent. Stir in the garlic, then the saffron-sherry mixture and the sherry drained from the raisins. Let cook until all the sherry evaporates. Let the mixture cool and then mix it with the chicken and pork, adding the bread crumbs, salt and pepper. Toast the pignoli nuts in a dry skillet over moderate heat until they are browned. Add these, too, to the meat mixture.

Place 2 ounces of the meat mixture into each cabbage leaf and fold the cabbage into little packages about 3 inches long and 1 inch thick. Roll the cabbage tightly and tie with twine to make neat packages.

Bring the chicken stock to a boil in a large pan. Add the cabbage rolls and let them simmer, partially covered, for about 45 minutes. The cabbage should be tender but still green. Correct the seasoning.

To serve, place two cabbage rolls, twine removed, in each heated soup plate, and cover them with stock garnished with dill leaves.

CAULIFLOWER MUSHROOM SOUP

Why are they called cauliflower mushrooms? Probably because, like cauliflower, they are yellowish white and can be separated into flowerlike sections. They look like huge bouquets of ruffled leaves, and are available only in the early autumn, which makes this soup necessarily seasonal. Luckily, it's quite as delicious when it's made with other wild mushrooms. The crepe, which can be made well in advance, is a nice addition to any thin soup.

CREPE:
6 egg yolks
2 tablespoons fresh bread
  crumbs
2 tablespoons grated
  Parmesan cheese
⅛ teaspoon ground sage
⅛ teaspoon white pepper
1 teaspoon olive or
  vegetable oil

SOUP:
10 ounces cauliflower
  mushrooms or other wild
  mushrooms

¾ pound, skinned and boned
  chicken breasts
Coarse salt
2 quarts Clarified Chicken
  Stock (page 105)
2 tablespoons olive or
  vegetable oil

Garnish:
½ cup thinly sliced scallions

To make the crepe, mix the egg yolks lightly, then stir in the bread crumbs, cheese, sage and pepper. Heat the oil in a heavy 12-inch skillet, wiping with a crumpled paper towel to make sure the surface is completely coated. Pour in the egg mixture, tilting the skillet so that it spreads to cover the entire surface. Let cook for 3 to 4 minutes over medium heat, or until it is firm and the upper surface glistens. Remove from the heat, and when the crepe is cool, run a knife around the edges to release it. Then roll the crepe into a very tight roll, cover with plastic wrap and set aside.

To make the soup, break the mushrooms into 8 florets and wash them. Cut the chicken breasts into julienne strips, pat dry and sprinkle with 1 teaspoon salt. Bring the clarified stock to a simmer in a large pot. Cut the crepe roll into ½-inch-wide slices at a slight angle. There should be about 24 pieces.

In a large skillet, heat 1 tablespoon of olive oil. Add the mushrooms and toss to brown them lightly. Transfer to the stockpot, leaving the oil behind. While the mushrooms simmer in the stock, for about 10 minutes, add the remaining oil to the skillet and sauté the chicken strips, tossing over high heat for a minute or two. Turn off the heat and let them remain in the skillet while you assemble the soup.

To serve, divide the chicken among heated soup plates with cauliflower mushroom and several slices of crepe. Ladle on the hot stock and garnish with scallions.

CHICKEN BOILED DINNER

Every country has a dish that combines a number of common ingredients in broth so the flavors intermingle. In France, it's *pot-au-feu*, in Spain, *cocido*, in Peru the Indian *sancochado* and in North America the New England boiled dinner. One of the most interesting of these boiled dinners comes from the Philippines, an Asian nation with strong ties with Spain. It's called *porchero manok*, and uses Spanish chorizo sausages with local bananas and vegetables. This is my version of the traditional recipe, one that cuts down the fat and shortens the time the vegetables are cooked.

2 Cornish game hens
Marinade:
  1 tablespoon Spanish paprika
  1 tablespoon brown sugar
  ¼ teaspoon cumin
  ⅛ teaspoon cayenne pepper
  1 tablespoon olive or
    vegetable oil
1 pound chorizos, about
  6 small sausages
8 small white onions, peeled
⅓ cup olive or vegetable oil

4 ripe platanos or unripened
  green bananas
About 2 quarts of water
2–3 teaspoons coarse salt
8 whole allspice
8 whole black peppercorns
10 ounces Brussels sprouts or
  1½ pounds green cabbage

Garnish:
  ⅓ cup chopped Italian
  parsley or cilantro

Dry the hens thoroughly. Discard the gizzards, truss, and place in a bowl. Make the marinade by mixing its ingredients, and coat the hens with it. Cut apart the linked chorizos, place in a saucepan with water and parboil for 10 minutes. Drain.

Cut a cross in the base of the onions. Heat the oil and brown the onions on all sides. Remove from the skillet. Place the hens in the pot and sear them on all sides over high heat. Remove and pour the fat from the pan. Put the drained chorizos into a large stockpot. Add the hens and onions. Prepare the platanos by cutting and discarding the pointed ends, then slicing each platano on the diagonal in three pieces. Pull away the skin and put all the pieces into the pot. Add just enough water to cover the contents of the pot. Add 2 teaspoons of salt, the allspice and peppercorns. Bring to a boil, partially cover, and simmer while you prepare the Brussels sprouts by cutting a cross in the base of each sprout or by cutting the cabbage into 8 wedges. If you prefer the sprouts, cook them separately in a pot of boiling salted water for 15 minutes, or until they are barely tender but still green. When the sausages and hens have simmered for 25 minutes, add the cabbage to the pot and cook for 10 to 20 minutes more, or until the cabbage is tender and the hens offer no resistance to the tip of a knife. Correct the seasoning.

To serve, work quickly to keep everything very hot. Remove the vegetables, sausages and hens with a slotted spoon. Remove the trussing strings and cut each bird into four pieces. Each serving should contain a quarter of a hen, a piece of sausage and equal amounts of platanos, onions and cabbage or Brussels sprouts. Ladle on some soup, and sprinkle with parsley or coriander.

CHICKEN-CABBAGE SOUP

If you cut the cabbage into hearty wedges, the soup will have a peasant-like texture to go with the flavors of tomato, garlic, basil and parsley. It's really a vegetable soup with a chicken garnish.

1½ pounds chicken breasts
3 tablespoons olive or
* vegetable oil*
2 onions, chopped (2 cups)
2 cloves garlic, minced
1 bay leaf
2 cups (about 1 pound) plum
* tomatoes, peeled, seeded and*
* chopped*
1 head green cabbage, about
* 2½ pounds*

7 cups Chicken Stock
* (page 105)*
2 teaspoons coarse salt

Garnish:
* ¼ cup chopped Italian*
*   parsley*
* ¼ cup thinly sliced basil*
*   leaves*

Skin and bone the chicken breasts. In a shallow pan with a lid, heat 1 tablespoon of the oil. Cook the onions over medium heat for about 5 minutes, or until they are translucent. Add the garlic, bay leaf and tomatoes. Lower the heat and cook, stirring frequently, for about 10 minutes, or until the mass is thickened.

Cut the cabbage in 8 wedges, *keeping the core* to retain the shape. Add to the pot. Pour on 5 cups of the chicken stock, bring to a boil, lower the heat and simmer, partially covered, for 10 minutes, or until the cabbage is barely tender.

Meanwhile, heat the remaining oil in a skillet and brown the chicken breasts over high heat. Transfer them to the cabbage pot and add the last 2 cups of stock and the salt. Bring back to a boil, lower the heat and poach the chicken for about 3 minutes. Remove the breasts from the pot and cut them into 8 pieces. Taste the broth and correct the seasoning.

To serve, divide the chicken and cabbage wedges among heated soup bowls. Ladle on the hot soup and garnish with parsley and basil.

CHICKEN AND CARACOLES

That is, snails; but I used the Spanish name to get you to read further. There's nothing wrong with canned snails, but if you can get fresh ones, the flavor will surprise you. The trick is to get rid of the unattractive gumminess before you use them. One way is to put the snails in a container with fennel tips for a week. It's faster to put them in a cardboard box with flour. The snails burrow through the flour, spitting it out and cleansing themselves as they go. Then you rinse them and blanch them for 5 minutes in boiling water, and the snails will be at the point that canned snails are when you buy them. It takes only a day or two, but you have to make sure you put a weight on the lid of the box, or you'll find snails all over the walls and ceiling of your kitchen.

1 15-ounce can snails or
1½ cups fresh blanched
snails
Marinade:
  ¼ cup bourbon
  3 tablespoons minced garlic
  1 teaspoon salt
  ¼ teaspoon sugar
1½ pounds chicken legs and
  thighs
2 teaspoons salt
1 tablespoon Spanish paprika
1 tablespoon olive or
  vegetable oil

4 medium onions, chopped
  (3 cups)
¼ teaspoon ground cloves
¼ teaspoon ground cumin
¼ cup flour
6 cups Chicken Stock
  (page 105)
3 cups cooked or canned
  red kidney beans, drained
White pepper
½ cup chopped Italian parsley

Drain the snails and rinse under cold running water. Make a marinade of bourbon, garlic, salt and sugar and toss the snails in it. Set aside while you prepare the soup.

Cut each chicken thigh in three pieces across the bone, each leg in two. Dry the chicken and rub with a mixture of 1 teaspoon salt and 1 teaspoon paprika.

In a large skillet, heat the oil and brown the chicken. Remove and set aside. Add the onions and cook for 5 minutes until golden. Add the cloves, cumin and remaining paprika to the pan, stirring over low heat for about 2 minutes. Add the snails in their marinade and cook and stir until the liquid evaporates. Stir in the flour and cook for 2 to 3 minutes. The mixture will be very thick. Pour in the chicken stock, a cup at a time, stirring until all 6 cups have been added. Bring to a boil and add the chicken pieces with their juices, the kidney beans and 1 teaspoon of salt. Simmer, covered, for 15 minutes, or until the chicken is quite tender. Add white pepper and taste for seasoning. Add the parsley as you remove the pot from the heat.

To serve, ladle into heated bowls, dividing the snails, chicken, red beans and soup among them.

CHICKEN AND CHORIZO SOUP

Chorizos are Spanish sausages, reddish from Spanish paprika, piquant rather than spicy. You can find them everywhere nowadays, but they are not always of top quality. When you shop for chorizos, remember that the softest sausages are the freshest. Herbs complement their taste wonderfully—especially, and unexpectedly, fresh basil.

6 ounces chorizo sausages
2 pounds chicken legs and thighs, cut into 1-inch pieces through the bones
2 tablespoons coarse salt
1 tablespoon olive or vegetable oil
1 large onion, chopped
1 cup peeled, seeded and chopped tomatoes (2 or 3 tomatoes)

1 tablespoon Spanish paprika
⅛ teaspoon cayenne pepper
¼ cup flour
7 cups Chicken Stock (page 105)
1 cup peas, fresh or frozen
White pepper

Garnish:
  1 cup thinly sliced basil leaves

Slice the chorizos into ⅛-inch rounds and set aside. Dry the pieces of chicken and sprinkle with 1 teaspoon of salt. In a large skillet, heat the oil and add the chicken. Sauté for 8 to 10 minutes, or until they are nicely browned on all sides. Remove them to a plate. Add the onion to the skillet and cook until browned. Stir in the tomatoes and cook for 5 minutes before adding the paprika and cayenne pepper. Sprinkle the flour over the tomato mixture. Stir to incorporate it and cook 2 minutes more. Then add the chicken stock, a cup at a time, stirring constantly. When all the stock is added, return the chicken pieces with their juices to the pot, along with the sliced chorizos and remaining salt. Bring to a boil, lower the heat and simmer for 15 to 20 minutes, or until the meat is tender.

If you use fresh peas, cook them in salted water while the soup is simmering. If you use frozen peas, defrost them, then drop into the soup for the last minute of cooking. Add white pepper and more salt to taste.

To serve, ladle the soup into heated plates, dividing the chicken and chorizos among the servings. Garnish with sliced basil leaves.

CHICKEN-GINGER SOUP

I love the clean, bright taste of ginger: you may have noticed that I've put it everywhere in this book. In this soup the ginger actually functions as a vegetable. I thought that for once I would have enough ginger, but for me it still wasn't too much.

1 3-pound chicken
Marinade:
  ⅔ cup beer
  Juice of 1 lemon
  3 cloves garlic, crushed
¼ pound fresh ginger
3 teaspoons salt
2 tablespoons olive or vegetable
  oil

8 cups water

Garnish:
  2 tablespoons chopped Italian
    parsley
  Croutons (optional)

Prepare the chicken, or have the butcher do it for you, by disjointing it, chopping each leg-with-thigh into 4 pieces, each breast into 3 pieces and each wing in half—18 pieces in all.

Mix the beer, lemon juice and garlic, add the chicken, and marinate for 1 hour at room temperature. Meanwhile, pare the ginger and cut it in julienne strips about 2 inches long. You should have ¾ to 1 cup. Cover with cold water and set aside.

Remove the chicken from the marinade, drain and wipe dry, brushing off any garlic that clings to the skin. Rub the dry chicken with 1 teaspoon of the salt. Strain the marinade through cheesecloth, squeezing to extract the juice. Set aside.

In a large skillet, heat 2 tablespoons oil. Brown the chicken over high heat for about 8 minutes. If necessary, do it in two batches. Remove, leaving the oil in the pan. Drain and dry the ginger. Add to the skillet and stir for 3 minutes, or until it becomes limp and starts to stick to the pan. Pour in the strained marinade and cook over medium heat until it has cooked down to half its volume. Then pour in the water, bring to a boil and lower the heat. Simmer for 10 minutes. Remove from the stove and skim off the fat with a spoon or blot the surface with paper towels.

Return the pan to the stove. Add the chicken pieces with the remaining salt. Bring back to a boil, lower the heat and simmer until the chicken is tender.

To serve, divide the chicken and ginger among heated soup plates. Ladle in the hot soup and sprinkle with freshly chopped parsley, and with croutons if you like.

CHICKEN HAMBURGESE, OR CHICKEN DUMPLING SOUP

"Hamburgese" refers to the tasty little dumplings flavored with bacon, pistachios and a breath of cumin that cook in your chicken stock.

¾ pound skinned and boned chicken breasts
¼ pound bacon
½ cup minced onion
½ teaspoon minced garlic
1½ ounces shelled pistachios, chopped
1 heaping teaspoon green peppercorns
1 teaspoon minced ginger

⅛ teaspoon ground cumin
⅛ teaspoon ground cinnamon
2 teaspoons coarse salt
1 cup fresh soft bread crumbs
8 cups Chicken Stock (page 105)

Garnish:
½ cup chopped Italian parsley

Grind the chicken meat in a grinder or chill it for 10 minutes and chop it as fine as you can with a sharp knife. (A food processor won't give the right texture.) Cut the bacon in ½-inch pieces and cook until crisp. Drain and reserve the fat in a bowl. Dry the bacon on a paper towel.

Place 1½ tablespoons of bacon fat in a skillet, and when it is hot, cook the onion and garlic until the onion is translucent. Add the pistachios and cook for 2 to 3 minutes. Scrape the mixture into a bowl. Let cool and then mix in the ground chicken.

Chop the green peppercorns and mix them with the ginger, cumin, cinnamon and salt. Add to the chicken mixture with another tablespoon of the bacon fat and the bread crumbs, mixing thoroughly with your hands to distribute the spices well.

Heat the chicken stock in a large pot. Meanwhile, form small oval dumplings about 1½ inches long from the chicken mixture. There should be 24 to 30 dumplings. When the soup has come to a boil, turn down to simmer and drop in the dumplings, a few at a time, and let them cook 3 minutes. Taste one for doneness: it should be slightly firm. Taste the stock and correct the seasoning.

To serve, divide the dumplings among heated soup plates. Ladle on the hot soup and garnish with reserved bacon bits and chopped parsley.

CHICKEN-MANGO SOUP

A beautifully colored soup to serve at the start of a meal. Mangoes grow on the West Coast and in South America, and now can be bought all over the country pretty much year-round. When you shop for mangoes, remember that riper is better, and even mushy mangoes are full of flavor. The skins are edible but tough, useful only for jams and chutneys. Scrape the meat out and then discard them.

¾ pound skinned and boned
  chicken breasts
Marinade:
  1 tablespoon raspberry
    vinegar
  1 tablespoon olive or
    vegetable oil
  1 teaspoon salt
2 ripe mangoes, 7 ounces each

1 onion, peeled and cut in
  1-inch squares (1 cup)
5 cups hot Chicken Stock
  (page 105)
½ pound chayote, bitter melon
  or broccoli stems, pared and
  diced (1 cup)
2 teaspoons coarse salt

Cover the chicken breasts with waxed paper and chill for 10 minutes in the freezer before cutting into 1- by 1½-inch pieces. Combine the marinade ingredients and marinate the chicken as you prepare the other ingredients.

Peel and pit one of the mangoes, chop and pass through a food mill or sieve set over a bowl. Set aside. Peel the other mango and cut into ½-inch cubes. Set aside.

Heat the oil in a large skillet and quickly toss the chicken over high heat. *Do not overcook*: the chicken should be opaque, but not at all browned. Remove to a plate with a slotted spoon and keep warm.

Sauté the onion in the oil remaining in the skillet. When it is soft, add the stock and vegetable, bring to a boil and simmer for 5 minutes, or until the vegetable is tender. Remove 1 cup of the stock, combine with the puréed mango and stir back into the soup. Bring back to the boil before dropping in the reserved mango cubes, leaving them in just long enough to heat through. Season with salt.

To serve, divide the still-warm chicken pieces among the heated soup bowls, then ladle on the broth, vegetable and mango.

CHICKEN AND SHIITAKE

Shiitake, or oak mushrooms, are the fresh version of Chinese dried black mushrooms. You can use dried mushrooms in place of some of the shiitakes in this soup, but you'll have to soak them in warm water first. It's hard to say how long this will take—some take 30 minutes, some several hours. The best way to tell if the mushrooms are ready is to squeeze them and see if they're soft all the way through. Or cut them lengthwise and look for dry spots in the center. It's better to oversoak than to undersoak. Even so, after you rinse the mushrooms, you must cut away the stems. They will never become really tender.

*1 pound skinned and boned
  chicken breasts
Marinade:
  1 tablespoon olive oil
  1 tablespoon sherry or wine
    vinegar
  1 teaspoon salt*

*1 pound shiitake
2 tablespoons oil
1 large onion, minced
7 cups Chicken Stock
  (page 105)
1–2 teaspoons coarse salt
½ cup chopped Italian parsley*

Chill the chicken for 10 minutes in the freezer, then cut into julienne strips ⅛ to ¼ inch thick. Mix the olive oil, vinegar and salt in a large bowl, add the julienned chicken and marinate for 10 minutes. Julienne the mushrooms and set aside.

Heat a large wok over medium-high heat. Pour in 2 tablespoons oil, and when it is very hot, stir-fry the chicken until the pieces turn opaque. Remove to a platter and keep warm. To the opaque liquid in the wok, add the minced onion and stir until it turns soft. Add the chicken stock and mushrooms and bring to a boil. Lower the heat and cook for 10 minutes, skimming off the scum that rises to the top. Correct the seasoning. Just before serving, stir in the parsley and the chicken.

To serve, divide the chicken among heated soup plates, ladling on the mushrooms and broth.

CHICKEN AND PEPPER SOUP

This soup is brilliantly colored, with the bright sweet taste of peppers. You can assume that the larger a pepper is, the milder its taste will be, and the riper it is, the sweeter it will be. Red peppers are simply ripe green peppers; now we also have beautiful hybrids in yellow and purple.

2 pounds chicken legs and thighs, cut in 2-inch pieces across the bone
2 teaspoons coarse salt
1 tablespoon olive or vegetable oil
1 large onion, cut in ¾-inch squares
3 garlic cloves, minced
1 bay leaf
1 tablespoon Spanish or regular paprika

3 tablespoons red wine vinegar
¼ cup flour
7 cups Chicken Stock (page 105)
2–3 sweet red peppers, seeded and cut in ¾-inch squares
2–3 sweet green peppers, seeded and cut in ¾-inch squares
8 new potatoes
Coarse salt and white pepper

Dry the chicken pieces and sprinkle with 1 teaspoon of the salt. Heat the oil in a large skillet and thoroughly sear the chicken until it is as browned as possible. Remove and set aside. Scrape the pan to loosen any brown bits on the bottom, then add the onion and sauté for 5 minutes before stirring in the garlic, bay leaf, paprika and vinegar. Stir to combine the vinegar and scrape up all the brown bits. Cook another minute or two.

Sprinkle on flour and stir. The mixture will be very thick. Add the chicken stock, a cup at a time, stirring until the mixture is smooth. Once the stock is smooth, add the remaining teaspoon of salt and return the chicken and its juices to the pot. Cover and simmer for 5 minutes. Add the pepper squares and cook until the chicken is done and the peppers, while still retaining their bright colors, have softened.

While the soup cooks, pare the potatoes and cook in salted water for 15 minutes. Drain and keep hot. Remove the finished soup from the stove and correct the seasoning with more salt and white pepper to taste. Discard the bay leaf.

To serve, ladle the soup into heated plates, dividing the chicken and peppers evenly and adding a hot potato to each bowl.

CHICKEN-VEGETABLE SOUP

A very thick soup, like a stew. If the directions to cut the onions in squares and the calabaza in cubes seem finicky, do it anyway. I promise you that the extra care makes the soup much better-looking.

2 pounds chicken legs and thighs
2 teaspoons coarse salt
1 tablespoon vegetable oil
2 medium Spanish onions, cut in ½-inch squares (1½ cups)
⅛ teaspoon nutmeg
¼ teaspoon cumin
1 fresh hot jalapeño pepper, seeded and minced

1 cup cooked or canned chick-peas
6 cups Chicken Stock (page 105)
1½ cups calabaza (or butternut squash), pared and cut in ½-inch cubes
½ pound escarole, mustard greens or spinach
1 tablespoon olive oil

Dry the chicken and sprinkle with 1 teaspoon of the salt. In a large skillet, heat the oil and brown the chicken well. Remove and pour off all but 2 tablespoons of accumulated fat. Add the onions, nutmeg and cumin to the pan, stirring and cooking for 4 minutes, or until the onions are soft. Stir in the pepper. Mash 2 tablespoons of the chick-peas and stir this into the skillet before you add the remaining chick-peas. The mixture will be very thick. Add the stock, the remaining teaspoon of salt, the chicken pieces and calabaza. Bring to a boil, lower the heat and simmer, partially covered, for about 10 minutes, or until the chicken is tender.

Wash the greens and discard any tough stems. Heat the olive oil in a wide skillet, and when it is hot, toss the greens about until they begin to wilt. Stir into the hot soup.

To serve, divide the chicken pieces among heated bowls, and fill each bowl with a ladleful of calabaza, chickpeas, greens and stock.

CHICKEN-WALNUT SOUP

A comforting, sweet soup, flavored only with salt and pepper. It has to be made at the last moment, but the only thing at all tedious in the preparation is removing the walnut skins. Do it ahead of time by soaking the nuts in boiling water for a few minutes, then rubbing with a towel. The longer they soak, the easier they are to peel.

*¾ pound skinned and boned
    chicken breasts
⅓ cup milk
1½ slices soft white bread,
    crusts removed
3 ounces shelled and skinned
    walnuts
6 cups Chicken Stock
    (page 105)
2 teaspoons coarse salt*

*¾ cup farina or Cream of
    Wheat
Coarse salt and white pepper
    to taste
1 tablespoon vegetable oil*

*Garnish:
    1 ounce shelled and skinned
        walnuts, chopped*

Wrap the chicken in waxed paper and place in the freezer to firm up slightly. Combine the milk and bread in a small bowl, and let the bread absorb most of the milk. Drop the skinned walnuts into a blender and chop briefly before adding the bread-milk mixture. Blend until the mixture is a smooth mass and set aside.

Bring the chicken stock and 1 teaspoon of the salt to a boil. Pour in the farina, stirring constantly. When the gruel begins to thicken, lower the heat and simmer about 10 minutes.

Cut the chilled chicken breasts into strips ½ inch wide and 2 inches long. Dry with a paper towel and sprinkle with the remaining teaspoon of salt.

Stir the blended walnut-bread mass into the farina and cook together for 2 minutes. The soup should now be quite thick and smooth, with a texture not unlike that of baby food. Correct the seasoning with more salt and white pepper to taste, cover the pan and keep warm.

Heat the oil in a skillet or wok. When it is hot, stir-fry the chicken pieces for 2 minutes over high heat, or until chicken turns opaque. Do not overcook.

To serve, fill heated soup plates with the soupy farina. Divide the chicken among the servings and sprinkle each bowl with chopped walnuts.

MAR Y MONTAÑA

That is, "sea and mountain," like the "surf and turf" served in steak houses. This combination of seafood and meat is deeply rooted in the food culture of the Iberian peninsula. Just think of paella, with its rabbit, chicken, clams and shrimp all cooked together with rice.

1 3-pound chicken
1 teaspoon paprika combined
with ½ teaspoon coarse salt
3 tablespoons olive oil
16 medium-large shrimps
(1 pound)
¾ teaspoon ground cumin
combined with ½ teaspoon
coarse salt
2 leeks, split and chopped
1 large clove garlic, minced
1 hot pepper, seeded and
chopped
1 medium tomato, peeled,
seeded and chopped

1 cup white wine
7 cucumbers, pared, seeded and
puréed in a blender
(3½ cups purée)
2½ cups water
2 teaspoons coarse salt
White pepper

Garnish:
1 tomato, peeled, seeded and
chopped
Chopped fresh coriander
leaves

Cut the chicken in 10 parts, cutting each leg-and-thigh into 3 pieces, each breast-and-wing into 2 pieces. Dry and rub with the mixture of paprika and salt. Heat 1 tablespoon of the oil in a large skillet and brown the chicken well. This will take about 10 minutes. Remove to a plate.

Remove all but the two lower shell segments and tail of each shrimp. Devein, rinse and pat dry. Pour off all but 2 tablespoons of fat from the skillet, sprinkle the shrimp with cumin and salt, and sauté for about 3 minutes, or until they turn pink. Remove to a plate.

To the small amount of highly spiced oil in the pan, add the remaining olive oil and cook the leeks over medium heat for about 3 minutes, or until they begin to wilt. Add the garlic, hot pepper and the chopped tomato. Cook another 3 minutes. Pour in the wine and cook until it reduces by half. Add the cucumber purée, bring to a boil, reduce the heat and simmer for 5 to 10 minutes, or until its raw taste has disappeared. The soup will taste flat when the cucumber is first added. This changes as the mixture simmers. Add the water, 2 teaspoons of salt and white pepper to taste. Bring back to the boil, reduce the heat, cover and simmer for 8 minutes. Return the shrimp and chicken, with their juices, to the pan and cook only long enough to heat them through.

To serve, place 2 shrimp and a piece or two of chicken in each heated soup plate and ladle the hot soup over all. Garnish with the chopped tomato and coriander.

CHICKEN-MUSSEL SOUP

Mussels have a rich, definite taste that goes well with chicken. Try to find fresh thyme if you can, and pull the leaves off the stems for a taste that can't be duplicated by dried thyme.

*4 small chicken legs with
    thighs (2–2½ pounds)*
24 mussels (1½ pounds)
8 new potatoes
*2½ quarts Chicken Stock
    (page 105)*
1 large Bermuda onion

*3 tablespoons olive or
    vegetable oil*
*2 tablespoons fresh thyme
    leaves*

Cut each leg-and-thigh into 3 pieces across the bone and refrigerate. Clean the mussels following the instructions for Mussel Bisque (page 54). Pare the potatoes and place in a large pot. Add the chicken stock and bring to a boil over moderate heat, skimming off the scum that rises to the surface. Let the potatoes cook in the stock for 10 minutes, or until slightly underdone. While the potatoes are cooking, peel the onion, slice, and separate into rings.

In an 11- or 12-inch skillet, heat 2 tablespoons of the oil and cook the chicken over high heat, turning the pieces until they are quite browned. Using tongs, transfer the chicken to the soup pot and simmer for about 5 minutes.

Quickly sauté the onion rings in the remaining oil. When they are barely browned but still retain some crunch, add them to the soup pot. Add the thyme leaves and mussels, cover the pot and let the mussels steam for 2 or 3 minutes, or until they open.

To serve, place 3 mussels, 1 or 2 chicken pieces, a potato and some onion rings in each preheated bowl, then cover with a generous ladleful of mussel-flavored stock.

CHICKEN MARMITAKO

This soup comes from San Sebastian, in Basque country. The Basques live in the mountains, where they raise cattle and poultry, but they are also near the sea, and their food often combines meat or chicken with seafood.

4 small chicken legs and
  thighs (1½–1¾ pounds)
16 medium shrimp or
  8 small crawfish
4 tablespoons olive or
  vegetable oil
1 16-ounce can Italian plum
  tomatoes
1 cup finely chopped onion
1 small carrot, diced (½ cup)
2 teaspoons minced garlic
1 tablespoon fresh thyme or
  ⅛ teaspoon dried thyme

7 cups Chicken Stock
  (page 105)
2 medium fennel bulbs
16 sea scallops
2 teaspoons coarse salt

Garnish:
  ¼ cup chopped Italian
    parsley or 2 tablespoons
    chopped fresh thyme

Cut each leg-and-thigh into 3 pieces with a cleaver. Remove all but the last two shell segments from the shrimp, leaving the tails on. Devein, rinse and dry the shrimp.

In a large skillet, heat 2 tablespoons of the oil and cook the chicken over moderate to high heat until browned on all sides. Pass the tomatoes through a food mill or strainer and set aside. When the chicken is cooked, remove it from the pan. Discard any remaining oil and wipe out the pan with a paper towel. Now add the remaining 2 tablespoons of oil, heat and sauté the onion and carrot in it for about 10 minutes. Stir in the garlic and thyme leaves and cook together briefly. Add the tomatoes and simmer for another 10 minutes, or until the mixture is quite thick.

Add the chicken stock and bring to a boil. Cut the fennel in quarters and simmer in the soup for 15 minutes, or until the fennel begins to soften. Return the cooked chicken to the pan and cook for another 10 minutes, or until it is very tender. When you are nearly ready to eat, add the shrimp or crawfish to the soup and let them cook for about 4 minutes, or until they turn bright red. Just before you eat, drop in the scallops. They will take only a minute to firm up in the hot broth. Add the salt to taste.

To serve, place a crawfish or 2 shrimp, 2 scallops and 1 or 2 pieces of chicken in each plate. Ladle on the hot soup and garnish with chopped parsley or a pinch of fresh thyme. Serve with a knife, fork and soup spoon and a side dish to receive the shells and bones.

FOUR-ALMOND SOUP, OR POLLO EN LOS ALMENDROS

Three of the almonds are actually differently cut ordinary almonds. The fourth is a different thing altogether: bitter almonds are hard to find, being used mainly to make flavoring oils. Apricot kernels make a good substitute, and can be found in Chinese and Hungarian markets. This is an especially simple soup to make, and very rewarding to eat.

¼ cup olive or vegetable oil

Scant ¼ cup slivered blanched
  almonds

Scant ¼ cup thinly sliced
  blanched almonds

Scant ¼ cup bitter almonds or
  apricot kernels

1 small Bermuda onion

Scant ¼ cup whole blanched
  almonds

2 tablespoons Amaretto liqueur

6 cups Chicken Stock
  (page 105)

2 teaspoons coarse salt

2 cups cubed potatoes
  (4 or 5 potatoes)

3 whole chicken breasts,
  skinned and boned and cut
  into 4 pieces each

White pepper

In a skillet, heat 1½ teaspoons of the oil and toss the slivered almonds over moderate heat until they are golden. Set aside to use as a garnish. Wipe the skillet with a paper towel. Heat another 1½ teaspoons of the oil and toast the thinly sliced almonds in the same manner, setting them aside to use as a garnish too.

Grind the bitter almonds or apricot kernels in a blender or a Mouli grater. Then measure out 2 teaspoons, saving the rest to use another time. Peel the onion, cut in half lengthwise, and then cut into rectangular shapes the size of almonds.

In a large skillet, heat 1 tablespoon of the oil and toss the onion in the pan until it begins to turn translucent. Add the whole almonds and sauté, stirring, until they are golden. Add the 2 teaspoons of ground bitter almonds, lower the heat and cook for a minute. Then add the Amaretto and let simmer until the liquid evaporates. Add the chicken stock, 2 teaspoons salt and potatoes and bring to a boil. Lower the heat and simmer, partially covered, for about 10 minutes, or until the potatoes are tender.

When nearly done, heat the remaining oil in another skillet. Dry the chicken pieces, sprinkle with salt and cook over moderate to high heat until they are golden and firm to the touch. Do not overcook. Remove from the heat and cover. Add white pepper, taste the soup and correct the seasoning.

To serve, place a piece of chicken in each soup bowl, and ladle on some broth with potatoes and almonds. Garnish each dish with some of the slivered almonds and some of the sliced almonds.

PHEASANT AND PEAR SOUP

Now that we only have to go to the butcher to buy cleaned, plucked pheasant, this romantic bird has become easy to cook. Gone are the days when you would have argued about how long to "hang" the bird after it was shot—three days or three weeks. Gone, even, are the days when skillful cooks would remove a whole pheasant skin with its feathers and drape it, like a blanket, over the soup tureen so that the guests could enjoy the beauty of the bird in full plumage. Think of that when you prepare this elegant soup.

1 2½-pound pheasant
3 tablespoons vegetable oil
¼ cup pear brandy, preferably
 Poire William
3 quarts Chicken Stock
 (page 105)
1 3-inch stick cinnamon
3 or 4 green Bosc pears,
 pared and diced

1 or 2 Bermuda onions, peeled,
 separated into layers, then
 cut into ¾-inch squares
 (3 cups)
½ teaspoon sugar
⅛ teaspoon ground cloves

Cut up the pheasant, removing the breast meat and leaving the legs and thighs in one piece. In a large skillet, heat 1 tablespoon of oil and brown the legs on both sides. Add the breast bones, neck, wings, gizzard and, if you have it, the head. Stir them about in the pan to brown. Add 2 tablespoons of the pear brandy and cook until it evaporates. Pour on the chicken stock and add the cinnamon stick. Bring to a boil, lower the heat and simmer for 45 to 60 minutes, skimming the surface as necessary.

When the leg meat is tender, remove the legs and strain the stock through a cheesecloth-lined sieve. Discard the debris and return the liquid to the pot. Add the pears and let them simmer for about 20 minutes, or until they are almost tender.

Cut the meat off the legs in fairly large chunks. Discard the bones. When the pears are ready, return the meat to the pot.

Meanwhile, heat 1 tablespoon of oil in a small skillet and cook the onion pieces over moderate heat until they begin to wilt. Sprinkle them with the sugar and cloves and cook until they are glazed. Scrape into the simmering soup and deglaze the pan with the remaining pear brandy, adding this, too, to the soup pot.

Wipe out the skillet and heat the remaining oil. Cut the pheasant breast in 2 pieces and brown. Do not overcook. Cut each breast half in 3 parts, and drop all 6 pieces into the stock just before you are ready to eat.

To serve, ladle the hot soup into preheated plates with equal amounts of pear, onion and browned pheasant meat.

SQUAB QUENELLES IN GARLIC BROTH

Quenelles, once so hard to make, have become simple since the advent of the food processor. Here, squab or other game birds are boned and the meat is marinated and combined with cream to make light and delicate meat dumplings. Make every effort to debone not only the breasts, but any other meaty scraps to make the ¾ pound of meat that the recipe calls for. You can, of course, simply buy enough chicken breast to make ¾ pound when it is boned. Be sure to save the bones, though.

3 squabs, 1¼ pounds each
Marinade:
  2 tablespoons brandy
  1 shallot, peeled and minced
  3–4 fresh sage leaves, chopped, or ⅛ teaspoon dried sage
  ¼ teaspoon ground cumin
  ⅛ teaspoon white pepper
  1½ teaspoons coarse salt

Stock:
  Bones and scraps from the squabs
  2 tablespoons pork fat
  2 whole bulbs garlic
  2 medium carrots, coarsely chopped

1 stalk celery, including green tops, coarsely chopped
1 onion, chopped
3–4 sprigs fresh thyme
1 bay leaf
2½–3 quarts water
Coarse salt and white pepper
2 tablespoons sweet sherry
1 cup heavy cream
4 tablespoons crushed ice
1 cup chopped Italian parsley leaves
1 cup chopped dill leaves

Garnish:
  Pasta bow ties, cooked al dente and drained

Before boning the squabs, combine the brandy, shallot, sage, cumin, pepper and salt in a bowl for the marinade.

Bone each squab by cutting it down the back. Reserve the liver, cut the gizzard in half and set the gizzard and heart to one side. Turn so the breast faces upward. Loosen the skin at the base of the second joint and at the wing ends. Remove the skin on both sides of the breast, using a small knife and your fingers to pull the skin from the meat. Cutting against the bone, cut out the breast meat. This is the main source of meat, and any way you bone it will be all right, as long as you get out all you can. Cut and scrape away any meat from the bones. The meat from the second joint can be used, but the leg has too many tendons to make boning worthwhile. As you work, drop the pieces in the bowl of marinade. When all three squabs are boned you should have ¾ pound of meat. Toss it in the marinade, cover the bowl and refrigerate.

Chop the breast bones, heads and necks in half. Dry the bones and gizzards with paper towels and brown them in pork fat in a large skillet. Transfer to a stockpot and then brown the vegetables and herbs in the fat. Add them to the stockpot, rinse out the skillet with a little water, and then add 2½ to 3 quarts water to the pot. Bring to a boil, lower the heat and simmer for 45 minutes to 1 hour, skimming the surface to remove any scum. Strain the stock, discard the bones and vegetables and skim off as much fat as you can. Add salt, pepper and sherry. There should be 8 or 9 cups of broth. The soup can be prepared up to this point and refrigerated ahead of time.

Transfer the squab with its marinade to the bowl of the food processor. Add the cream and crushed ice and process until you have a smooth, cohesive mass. Scrape into a chilled bowl and refrigerate while you bring the strained broth back to the boiling point and reduce the heat so that it simmers.

Cover a jelly-roll pan with waxed paper and spread half the chopped parsley and dill over the surface. Take the quenelle mixture from the refrigerator. Using two small tablespoons, from the quenelles by mounding the mixture into an oval shape on one spoon, then pushing it off onto the parsley-dill mixture with the other spoon. When all the quenelles are formed and are resting on the waxed paper—there should be about 18— sprinkle the rest of the herbs over the top of them. Roll the dumplings gently to cover them completely with chopped herbs.

Drop the quenelles one at a time from a slotted spoon into the simmering stock and let each one poach for 3 to 4 minutes. Do not overcook.

Remove them, one at a time, and place them on a platter in one layer. Strain the stock, which will have a lot of herbs floating about in it. Wipe out the pot and reheat the broth, correcting the seasoning. Drop the precooked bow ties in the broth to heat them through, and lower in the quenelles to do the same.

To serve, ladle the broth in preheated soup plates, dividing the quenelles among the servings and adding 2 or 3 bow ties to each plate.

RABBIT AND WILD FENNEL SOUP

Fennel grows wild all over the United States. Once you start to look for it, you will see it growing along the sides of highways, especially in the Northwest. The dried sticks of fennel that float like little logs in this soup can also be found in shops that specialize in herbs.

1 2¾-pound rabbit, skinned

Marinade:
  3 cloves garlic, minced
  1 teaspoon coarse salt
  ½ teaspoon ground fennel
  1 teaspoon balsamic vinegar
3 tablespoons olive or
  vegetable oil
3 quarts Chicken Stock
  (page 105)
12 sticks dried wild fennel,
  cut in 4-inch lengths

1 large rutabaga or
  yellow turnip
1 head Savoy cabbage,
  1½–2 pounds
1 large onion
½ teaspoon sugar
Coarse salt and white pepper

Garnish:
  ½ cup chopped Italian
  parsley

Have the butcher cut the rabbit into 9 serving pieces and give you the rest of the rabbit to use in the stock.

Prepare the marinade by combining the garlic, salt and fennel with a mortar and pestle, then stirring in the vinegar. Rub the mixture into the rabbit pieces and let marinate for 1 hour.

In a large skillet, heat 2 tablespoons of the oil and sauté the rabbit, tossing the pieces over moderate heat for 10 minutes, or until they are quite browned. Remove from the skillet and wipe the rabbit to take off any burnt bits of marinade that may be sticking to the skin. Set aside.

Add 1 cup of the stock to the pan and bring to the boil, stirring to incorporate all the browned bits at the bottom of the skillet. Strain the stock through cheesecloth into a large stockpot with the rest of the chicken stock, the fennel sticks, the browned rabbit pieces and the reserved rabbit parts. Bring to a boil and simmer, covered, for about 1 hour. Skim the surface during the cooking to remove the scum and brown bits that rise to the top.

While the soup simmers, prepare the vegetables. Pare the rutabaga or turnip, cut it into 8 pieces, and "turn" or carve them into egg-shaped pieces. Trim the cabbage, discarding any discolored leaves, and cut into 8 wedges, leaving enough core to hold the wedges together. Separate the onion into layers and cut each layer into ¾-inch squares.

When the rabbit is cooked, remove all the extra parts used to enrich the stock and discard them. Add the rutabaga and cook for about 15 minutes. Lay the cabbage wedges on top of the soup and, in 5 minutes, when they begin to soften, press them down into the stock. Let cook 10 to 15 minutes.

Heat the remaining oil in a small skillet and cook the onion until it softens. Sprinkle with sugar and continue to cook until soft. Scrape into the soup and then deglaze the onion pan with a ladleful of the stock. Return this liquid to the pot. Now all the vegetables should be tender and the rabbit thoroughly cooked, nearly falling off the bone.

To serve, lift out the cabbage with tongs and place a wedge in each preheated soup plate with a piece of rabbit, rutabaga and one or two sticks of fennel. Ladle the hot soup into each plate and garnish with parsley.

ROULADE OF TURKEY SOUP

Some years ago I got the idea of turning small game birds, which have a small proportion of meat to bone, into roulades by boning them and chopping some of the meat into a flavorful stuffing. Here I've done it with a wild turkey, then poached, sliced and served the roll in a flavorful broth. You could use a small domestic turkey or capon. As a matter of fact, it's a great way to stretch other game birds, such as pheasant. The admittedly tricky technique makes the bird moister, easier to carve, and stretches it significantly. A 10-pound turkey, which would ordinarily feed eight scantily, serves twenty by this method. If you decide to try this recipe, do it over a couple of days. That will give you time to make the stock, marinate the stuffing and do the final rolling, poaching and cooling. If you have roulade left over, serve it up as a cold appetizer with cornichons and a hearty mustard.

1 wild turkey, 9½–10 pounds

Stock:
  Carcass, neck and bones of the turkey
  3 onions, skin on, quartered
  2 leeks with 2 inches of green, chopped
  2 large carrots, chopped
  6 stalks celery, including green leaves, chopped
  2 whole bulbs garlic, sliced in half horizontally
  6 quarts water
  12 peppercorns, crushed
  8 juniper berries
  3 whole cloves
  ½ teaspoon dried thyme
  10 sprigs fresh parsley

Stuffing:
  ⅓ cup brandy
  ½ cup dried apricots, chopped

¼ cup raisins
Gizzard
Reserved dark meat of turkey (about 1 pound)
1 pound fresh pork fat, ground
¼ tightly packed cup fresh bread crumbs
3 tablespoons coarse salt
1 teaspoon dried thyme
1 teaspoon dried marjoram
¼ teaspoon ground cumin
¼ teaspoon white pepper
Liver and heart, quartered

8 baby carrots
8 small white potatoes, pared
Coarse salt and white pepper

Garnish:
  Bunch of scallions or chives, thinly sliced

Have your butcher bone the turkey, saving all the bones, gizzard and bits of dark meat for you. Or follow the directions Jacques Pepin gives in *La Technique* (Harper and Row) for boning a chicken to make chicken sausage, Technique 90. Discard nothing. When you are done, cover the exposed surface of the bird with waxed paper, fold the turkey in half, then cover and refrigerate. To prepare the gizzard, cut away all the tough outer skin and cut the gizzard into quarters. Cut the heart and liver into four pieces. Refrigerate, adding any bits and pieces to the pile of bones set aside for stock.

MAKING THE STOCK. Preheat the oven to 450°. Cut the neck and carcass into several parts and place in a roasting pan with the other bones. Brown in the hot oven for 30 to 40 minutes, tossing now and then. When the bones are browned, add the onions, leeks, carrots, celery and garlic. If no fat has been released and the vegetables begin to stick to the pan, add a tiny bit of vegetable oil, just enough to coat the vegetables so they can be moved about. Lower the heat to 400° and brown the vegetables. Do not let them burn.

Scrape the bones and vegetables into a large stockpot. Use a cup or two of water to deglaze the roasting pan, then add the browned liquid to the stockpot, with enough water to cover the bones and vegetables by 2 inches. Add the peppercorns, juniper berries, cloves, thyme and parsley sprigs and bring to the boil. Lower the heat and simmer, partially covered, for 3 to 4 hours, never letting it come to a vigorous boil. Skim off any scum that rises to the top.

Remove the stockpot from the stove. When it is cool enough to handle, drain and discard the bones and measure the stock. There should be 4 to 5 quarts. Strain through a fine sieve lined with cheesecloth. Refrigerate.

MAKING THE STUFFING. Pour the brandy into a bowl and soak the apricots, raisins and gizzard for 30 minutes. Remove and reserve the gizzard. Using a meat grinder or food processor, grind the dark meat of the turkey. In a large bowl, combine the ground meat with the pork fat, bread crumbs and coarse salt. Add the thyme, marjoram, cumin and pepper with the marinated apricots, raisins and brandy. Cover and refrigerate for at least 8 hours to let the stuffing mellow.

ROLLING THE ROULADE. Cut a piece of cheesecloth about 26 inches square. Spread it on your work surface and lay the boned turkey, skin side down, on the cheesecloth so that the neck skin is to your left. The area closest to you should have a 1-inch margin of skin, while the side farthest from you should have 2 or 3 inches of free skin. Distribute the stuffing over the two-thirds of the surface nearest you, patting it into a 9-inch square. Leave the third of the surface farthest from you free of filling. Dot the pieces of gizzard, liver and heart over the stuffing.

Pick up the skin closest to you and begin to roll it over the stuffing. When you are half done, fold in the neck skin and the skin at the right end. Continue to roll tightly until the filling is almost enclosed, with the cheesecloth on the outside.

At this point, lift the cheesecloth and use it to turn the roulade, continuing until the free skin at the far side can be lifted to meet the roll and enclose it. Now twist 6 inches of cheesecloth at each end as tightly as possible. Grasping each end, roll the enclosed bird across your table in one direction only. Lift and return to the starting point and again roll in one direction. Do it about six times, until the roll has an even shape.

TYING THE ROULADE. Using twine, tie the twisted ends of the cheesecloth as close to the meat as you can. Make a tie at the center of the roll. Then make ties at 4-inch intervals on one side of the center and then the other. Although the roll will look compact after 8 ties, for a really good job you should go back and make ties between each of the original 8, so that there are 14 ties altogether in the 14-inch roll.

COOKING THE ROULADE. Select a pot long enough to hold the meat without bending it: a small fish poacher is ideal. Heat the stock in another pot just to the boiling point. Put the roulade in the fish poacher and cover with heated stock to the top of the roll. If there isn't enough stock, add some water. Return to the boil, lower the heat and barely simmer for 1½ hours, or until a thermometer inserted in the center of the roll reads 150°. Remove the pot from the stove and let the roulade cool until it is easy to handle. The meat will stay very hot for a couple of hours, so the roulade should be cooked several hours before you plan to serve the soup. This will also make slicing easier. While the meat cools, cook the carrots and potatoes in boiling water.

Remove the roulade from the stock. Put the stock back over a burner and simmer for about 15 minutes with the carrots and potatoes, or until they are done. Correct the seasoning with salt and white pepper to taste.

Meanwhile, cut the string, unroll the cheesecloth, and cut the roulade into ½-inch slices.

To serve, place a slice of roulade in each preheated soup plate. Ladle on the stock, and place a carrot and potato in each serving. Garnish with scallions or chives.

NOTE: If you have simmered the stock very gently, it should be quite clear. If, however, it has become cloudy, you can clarify it by using the egg-white technique described in the recipe for Clarified Chicken Stock, page 105. In this case, use only the egg whites and shells.

SQUAB AND BARLEY SOUP

When I was a child in Peru, my grandfather used to have squab every Sunday for dinner, often in a soup like this one. Squabs are baby pigeons less than a month old. They are technically wild birds, but now they are bred domestically and are available year-round.

3 squabs, 1–1¼ pounds each
¼ cup olive or vegetable oil
2½ quarts Chicken Stock
  (page 105)
1 medium onion, peeled and
  quartered
8 cloves garlic, peeled
12 sprigs fresh thyme
1 cup barley

1 large onion, chopped (2 cups)
1 small carrot, diced (½ cup)
2 stalks celery, diced (½ cup)
1 teaspoon coarse salt

Garnish:
  ⅓ cup chopped Italian
  parsley

Have the butcher prepare the squabs by cutting each bird into 2 breast pieces and 2 legs-with-thighs. Keep the necks, backs, wing tips and so forth for the stock.

In a heavy skillet, heat 2 tablespoons of the oil and thoroughly brown the stock pieces, *not the breasts and thighs,* for about 15 minutes.

Heat the chicken stock in a large pot. When the pieces of squab are browned, add them to the pot with the onion, garlic and thyme. Bring to a boil, reduce the heat and simmer for 45 minutes, skimming off any scum that rises to the surface. While the stock is cooking, simmer the barley in 3 cups of water, covered, for 45 minutes.

Strain out the bones and vegetables from the stock. There should be about 2½ cups of enriched broth.

In a skillet, heat 1 tablespoon of oil and sauté the chopped onion for 5 minutes. Scrape this into the stockpot and cook for a few minutes before you add the strained barley. Let the barley simmer for about 5 minutes, then add the diced carrot and celery. Cover the pot and turn off the heat while you cook the squabs. The carrots and celery will cook just enough to add an unexpected crunch to the soup.

Heat the last tablespoon of the oil in a large heavy skillet. Dry the squab breasts and thighs, sprinkle with 1 teaspoon of salt and brown them, skin side first. When that is a rich dark brown, turn and brown the flesh side. *Do not overcook*: squab should be rare and juicy.

Correct the seasoning of the broth, and stir in the parsley and the pieces of squab.

To serve, fill each bowl with the thick barley soup and put a piece of squab breast and leg in each serving. Provide a knife, fork and spoon and a small side dish for the bones.

SANCOCHADO DE CODORNIZ, OR QUAIL SOUP

Sancochado is a boiled dinner made by Peruvian Indians over an open fire. It usually includes potatoes, hot peppers and some sort of game. Although quail are tiny, their flesh is tough and responds well to braising or slow simmering in a soup.

8 quail, about ¼–½ pound each
1 teaspoon coarse salt
8 sprigs fresh thyme or ½ teaspoon dried thyme
8 tiny carrots or 2–3 medium carrots
8 new potatoes
8 Brussels sprouts

8 leeks, whites only
2½ quarts Chicken Stock (page 105)
White pepper

Garnish:
½ cup chopped Italian parsley

Wipe out the cavities of the quail with a damp towel. Handle the birds gently, as their skin tears easily. Rub the cavities with a little salt and then place a sprig of thyme or pinch of dried thyme in each. Truss the birds, tying the legs together and crossing the wings at the back.

Pare and trim the carrots. If you can't get baby carrots, cut the larger carrots into 8 pieces, shaping or "turning" them into long ovals. Pare and shape the potatoes the same way. Cut an X in the core of each Brussels sprout. Trim the leeks. All the vegetables should be delicate and perfect in appearance to complement the tiny quail.

Fill a 12-inch skillet with high sides with the chicken stock and bring to the point of boiling. Lower the quail into the simmering stock. They should be almost totally immersed. Poach them gently, skimming off any scum that rises to the surface. After 5 minutes, check the birds. They should be considerably softened. Add the potatoes and carrots and, after 5 minutes, the leeks. Cover the pan and cook the vegetables for 10 minutes more. Check the quail, which should now be nearly tender. Add the Brussels sprouts, partially cover the pot again, and cook for 5 more minutes, or until the sprouts, still green, begin to soften.

If at any time during this cooking, one of the vegetables appears to be done, it can be removed with a slotted spoon and returned to the pot later for a short reheating. This is true of the quail as well.

Remove the quail and cut away the trussing strings. Taste the broth and correct the seasoning.

To serve, place a quail in each preheated soup plate with a carrot, potato, a Brussels sprout and piece of leek. Ladle on the hot broth and garnish with parsley. Serve with a knife, fork, spoon and a small plate for the bones.

VENISON-CHESTNUT SOUP

A rich, winy soup that can be made with any of the big game: moose, elk or any variety of deer. It's a nice autumnal dish, a mixture of seasonal game, chestnuts and, if you can get them, wild mushrooms in whole or in part.

Marinade:
  1½ teaspoons ground savory
  1 teaspoon ground anise
  ¼ teaspoon ground cloves
  ¼ teaspoon white pepper
  ¼ cup sherry wine vinegar
  2 tablespoons Achiote Oil
    (see page 42) or
    1½ tablespoons olive oil
    mixed with 2 teaspoons
    paprika
  1 teaspoon minced garlic
  1 large onion, chopped
  1 large carrot, chopped
  (1 cup)

3 stalks celery, including
  leaves, chopped (¾ cup)
2-pound piece of venison from
  the neck or loin
60 fresh chestnuts, about
  1½ pounds
5 tablespoons pork or bacon fat
4 cups red wine
3 quarts water
8–12 sprigs parsley or thyme,
  tied together
1 pound mushrooms

Garnish:
  ⅓ cup chopped cilantro or
    Italian parsley

In a large bowl, combine the savory, anise, cloves and pepper and stir in the vinegar. Then add the oil, garlic, onion, carrot and celery. Cut the venison into 8 large pieces and toss with the marinade. Cover and let sit at room temperature at least 8 hours or refrigerate overnight.

To prepare the chestnuts, heat the oven to 425°. Slash the skin of each chestnut and place, slashed side up, on a baking sheet. Sprinkle with water and roast until the skins split open. This should take 15 to 20 minutes. When the chestnuts are cool enough to handle, peel off the hard outer skin and the thin inside skin, using a small paring knife. Divide the chestnuts: 36 for the initial cooking, 24 reserved to be added whole.

Remove the meat from the marinade and pat it dry. In a very large skillet, heat 2 tablespoons of the fat and sear the meat well. Remove from the pan. Stir in all the marinade and vegetables and cook for about 5 minutes. Pour in the wine and cook for 10 to 12 minutes, or until the wine reduces by a third. Add the water and 36 chestnuts and bring to a boil. Return the meat to the pan with the parsley or thyme and let the soup simmer for 1½ to 2 hours, or until all are tender. Skim off any scum that rises to the top. When done, remove from the stove, lift out the meat and remove and discard the parsley or thyme.

Blend the liquid, vegetables and chestnuts in a blender, a cup at a time, until it is a very smooth, thick purée. There should be about 2 to 2½ quarts.

Wipe out the skillet and heat the remaining 3 tablespoons fat. Pat the meat dry and sauté briefly to regain the original brown color. Remove, and toss the 24 reserved chestnuts in the fat until they take on color. Add the mushrooms and sauté together. Then pour in the purée and bring to a simmer. Add the meat and let the chestnuts, mushrooms and meat cook for 30 minutes more. Correct the seasoning.

To serve, fill preheated bowls with the rich, thick soup and mushrooms, seeing that each bowl has a large piece of venison and 3 chestnuts in it. Sprinkle with chopped herbs and serve with a knife, fork and spoon.

Cheese and Fruit Soups

CHAMPUS

I like to serve this nourishing soup, from Peru's Pacific coast, in the late afternoon, after a day of skiing. It's made with cherimoya, a sweet custardy fruit from Peru, or with guanabana, which originally came from Peru but is now grown in California and Florida. If you can't find either of these delectable South American imports, use the always available Bartlett pears.

1 3½-pound pineapple
2 quarts water
2 3-inch sticks cinnamon
10 whole cloves
1 or 2 fresh or dried hot peppers
½ cup sugar
1 teaspoon coarse salt
4 dried figs
6 pounds ripe cherimoya
  (about 7) or 6 pounds
  guanabana

1½ cups milk
2 1-pound cans white hominy,
  rinsed and drained
2 tablespoons sweet potato flour
  or 1 tablespoon cornstarch
2 ounces dried apricots,
  quartered
1 tart apple, peeled and diced
1 pear, peeled and diced
2 tablespoons black currants
½ cup heavy cream

Cut off and discard the top and bottom of the pineapple. Peel off the skin, wash it and set it aside. Cut the pineapple into four lengthwise pieces and slice off the cores.

In a saucepan, combine the water, cinnamon, cloves, peppers, sugar, salt and figs. Bring to a boil, lower the heat and simmer for 1 hour. Add the pineapple pulp, core and skin, return to the boil and simmer 45 minutes more. Remove the pineapple pulp and cinnamon sticks with a slotted spoon. Set aside the cinnamon sticks and cut the pineapple into ¾-inch cubes when it is cool enough to handle. Set aside.

Strain the broth through a strainer lined with cheesecloth. Squeeze the cheesecloth to extract all the flavor and discard the contents of the cheesecloth. You should have 1 quart of broth. If you have more, boil it down until you have the right amount; if you have less, add water.

Break the cherimoya in half with your hands and scrape out the pulp and seeds onto a plate with a tablespoon. Mash the pulp with a fork. Pick out the seeds and place them in a bowl. Continue with the rest of the cherimoyas until all the pulp and seeds are separated. Pour the milk into the bowl of seeds, stir and set aside.

Combine 2 cups of the hominy, the sweet potato flour (but not the cornstarch), 1½ cups of the cooked pineapple cubes and the fruit broth, and purée in the blender. Pour into a saucepan with the reserved cinnamon sticks, bring to a boil and simmer for 2 to 3 minutes. Add the remaining hominy, the remaining pineapple cubes, the apricots, apple, pear and currants and cook over low heat for 10 to 15 minutes. If you don't have sweet potato flour, mix the cornstarch with 2 tablespoons of cold water and stir into the soup at this point.

Now strain the cherimoya seeds and milk through cheesecloth, squeezing to extract all the flavor. Discard the seeds and pour the flavored milk into the soup. Return to the boil. Add 4 cups of cherimoya pulp and the cream and return nearly to the boiling point.

To serve, ladle the soup into preheated bowls. Put a spoonful of the remaining cherimoya pulp in the center of each bowl.

VARIATION: You can use pears in place of the cherimoya or guanabana. Instead of mashing the cherimoya and soaking the seeds in milk, peel, core and coarsely chop 2¼ pounds underripe Bartlett pears. There should be about 4 cups. Purée this in a blender with the milk and add to the soup after you have simmered the fruit broth, hominy and fruit for 10 to 15 minutes. Heat thoroughly but do not boil. Then add the cream and heat once again nearly to the boil.

To serve, garnish with a dollop of sour cream.

A CHEESE SOUP POSING
AS A BREAD

A wonderful presentation of soup, bread and tureen all in one. A milky soup thick with cheese and vegetables is served from a tureen made of a loaf of bread. When the soup is all ladled out, the guests can share the cheese-encrusted bread. A 3½-pound loaf of bread is the best size, big enough to hold all the soup. But if you can't find that size, you can use a 2-pound loaf and refill it; or use two 2-pound loaves and there will be twice as much bread for everyone.

*3- to 3½-pound round loaf of
    white Italian or Swiss bread*
*6–8 tablespoons olive or
    vegetable oil*
*2 cloves garlic, peeled and
    crushed*
¼–½ teaspoon coarse salt
¼ teaspoon cayenne pepper
1 small head cauliflower
1 bunch broccoli

1 small onion, chopped
¼ teaspoon ground nutmeg
Pinch of salt
*Pinch of cayenne or
    ¼ teaspoon white pepper*
2 quarts milk
1 bay leaf
8 ounces Gruyère, grated
8 ounces Jarlsberg, grated

Cut off the top of the bread with a serrated knife and set it aside. With a spoon, scoop out the bread, scraping the bottom and sides carefully so as not to break the crust. Use enough of the scooped-out bread to make 10 ounces or 5 cups of fresh bread crumbs. Set the rest aside for future use.

In a large skillet, heat 2 tablespoons of the oil with the garlic. Let the garlic barely turn color, and dump in 4 cups of the crumbs, stirring them until they dry out and become crisp and lightly browned. Remove and discard the garlic, sprinkle the crumbs with salt and cayenne and scrape them from the skillet onto paper towels to dry.

Prepare the cauliflower by breaking off the florets and paring the stalks. Wash, drain and set aside. Prepare the broccoli in the same manner. Then chop the pared cauliflower and broccoli stalks, blanch them for 1 minute in boiling water and drain.

In a large pan, heat 1 to 2 tablespoons of oil and sauté the onion until it softens and turns translucent. Stir in the nutmeg, pinch of cayenne and the remaining cup of bread crumbs, stirring briefly while they absorb the oil. Add the chopped stalks, milk and bay leaf, bring to a boil and simmer for 10 minutes. Remove from the heat, discard the bay leaf, then purée the mixture in a blender, a few cups at a time, until it is smooth. You should have about 9 cups of milky liquid. Pour this into the top of a double boiler with 6 ounces of each of the cheeses, reserving 2 ounces of each cheese.

Blanch the reserved cauliflower and broccoli florets in boiling water until they are just tender. Drain, drop into cold water to stop the cooking, and drain again.

Preheat the oven to 350°. Sprinkle the remaining 2 ounces of Gruyère and of Jarlsberg into the empty bread shell and press it against the bottom and sides with your fingers. Then brush the inside of the shell—including the inside of the lid—with the least amount possible of the remaining oil. Put the lid in place and set the bread in the oven to heat for 10 minutes, just long enough for the cheese to melt into the bread. This will form a protective barrier when it cools. Take the bread out of the oven and set it aside, leaving the oven lit.

While the bread is in the oven, reheat the soup and cheese only long enough for the cheese to melt and the soup to become fairly warm. Fill the now slightly cooled shell with the drained cauliflower and broccoli florets. Pour in the soup from the double boiler. Cover with the bread lid and return to the oven for 20 minutes, or until everything becomes piping hot. Don't let it stay in the oven any longer than is necessary, or the soup will thicken too much and the bread will become too crisp.

To serve, put the reserved toasted crumbs in a small serving bowl. At the table, ladle some cheesy soup with broccoli and cauliflower into each preheated soup plate, and sprinkle with crumbs. Pass the dish of crumbs around; they are so good that everyone always wants more. When the tureen is empty, let everyone tear off chunks of cheesy bread to eat with the soup.

COLD APPLE SOUP

Fresh apples give texture to soup, thickening it much as potatoes do. Of all the varieties, greenings are best for cooking. I think you'll find that green peppercorns add an interesting heat and perfume. Buy them fresh or canned; canned peppercorns will have to be drained and rinsed before you use them. The flavor of this soup improves with overnight chilling.

1 small carrot, chopped fine
3–4 sprigs fresh dill or parsley
1 sprig mint or ¼ teaspoon
   dried spearmint
8–10 whole black peppercorns
1 2-inch stick cinnamon
2 teaspoons green peppercorns
   (rinse and drain if using
   canned)
6 cups water
7 large green apples
1 tablespoon lemon juice
3 tablespoons vegetable oil

2 medium onions, chopped
   (1½ cups)
1½ tablespoons sugar
5 tablespoons Calvados
¼ teaspoon white pepper
Coarse salt

Garnish:
   5 tablespoons sour cream
   ½ teaspoon green
      peppercorns
   6–8 mint leaves

Tie the carrot, dill, mint, black peppercorns, cinnamon and green peppercorns in cheesecloth to make a bouquet garni. In a large saucepan, heat the water and bouquet garni and bring to a boil. Reduce heat and simmer for 25 minutes while you prepare the other ingredients.

Pare, quarter and seed the apples. Dice one apple for garnishing and toss with lemon juice. Just before the bouquet garni has finished simmering, drop the diced apple into the water, boil for 1 minute and remove with a slotted spoon or strainer. Reserve. Chop the remaining apples and drop into a bowl of water to which lemon juice has been added.

In a large saucepan, heat the oil and sauté the onions until they are translucent. Add the sugar and Calvados and cook until the brandy evaporates. Drain the unblanched apples and sauté them, stirring and tossing, for about 5 minutes. Scrape the contents of this pan into the pot containing the bouquet garni. Simmer for 5 to 10 minutes, or until the apples are completely soft. Turn off the heat and remove the bouquet garni, squeezing it over the pot to extract all the juices. Discard. Purée the soup in a blender or food processor until it is very smooth and creamy. Chill overnight.

To serve, correct the seasoning with pepper and more salt if necessary. Stir in the blanched apple cubes and pour into chilled soup bowls. Mix the sour cream and green peppercorns together and add a dollop to each serving, sticking the stem end of a mint leaf into each dollop.

MELON SOUP

Use honeydew, cantaloupe, cranshaw, Persian—any melon but watermelon. Plan ahead so that the soup can chill for at least 8 hours. If you don't have that much time, speed the process, as restaurant kitchens do, by fitting the bowl of soup into a larger container that holds ice, lots of salt and a little water: something like an ice cream freezer.

1 or 2 ripe honeydew melons,	*Pinch of coarse salt*
weighing 6½–7 pounds	*About 1 tablespoon sugar*
Pinch of cayenne pepper	*3 tablespoons heavy cream*
⅛ teaspoon ground mace	*8 sprigs fresh mint (optional)*

Quarter the melon. Remove and discard the seeds and cut 24 balls with a melon baller. Place them in a glass bowl, cover with plastic wrap and refrigerate.

Run a knife from tip to tip under the green part of each melon quarter, separating the pulp from the rind. Then cut the pulp into ½-inch slices. Discard the skin and purée the melon in a blender. Add the cayenne, mace, salt and sugar to the first batch, and transfer the purée to a bowl as each batch is finished. When all the melon is blended, stir to combine. Cover the bowl with plastic wrap and chill for 8 hours or overnight. When the purée is very cold, stir in the cream and add more sugar if it is needed.

To serve, fill chilled soup plates with the soup and drop 3 melon balls into the center of each plate. If you like, put a large sprig of mint on the serving plate beneath the soup plate.

NOTE: A blender is the best machine to use. If you don't have one, a food processor will do, but the soup won't be quite as smooth.

PEAR AND TURNIP SOUP

This soup has the bouquet and texture of pears with the peppery heat of turnips added to it. Green Bosc pears are best, but you can use any others that are in season. Turnips come two ways, white and yellow, and they are totally different. This is a recipe for the lighter, more watery, quicker-cooking white turnips. The surprise in this soup is the last-minute addition of honiny: not a gruel, but white corn kernels available in cans in Spanish food shops.

1 medium carrot, chopped
  (¾ cup)
1 fresh or dried hot green
  pepper, cut in half and
  seeded
1 sprig fresh tarragon or
  ¼ teaspoon dried tarragon
3 whole cloves
¼ teaspoon allspice
8 cups water
6 medium Bosc pears
  (2–2½ pounds)
1 tablespoon lemon juice or
  vinegar

1½ pounds white turnips
2 tablespoons butter
1 large onion, chopped
2 tablespoons sweet sherry
2 teaspoons coarse salt
6 tablespoons heavy cream

Garnish:
  1 cup hominy (white corn
    kernels), drained
  1 tablespoon butter
  Juice of 1 lemon
  6 sprigs fresh mint

Make a bouquet garni by tying the carrot, pepper, tarragon, cloves and allspice in a cheesecloth bag. Place in a saucepan with the water, bring to a boil, reduce heat and simmer while you prepare the other ingredients. When ready to use it, measure the liquid: there should be 6 cups. Add more water if necessary to make this amount.

Pare, seed and chop the pears, dropping them in a bowl of water to which you have added lemon juice or vinegar. Pare and chop the turnips and set aside.

In a skillet, heat the butter and sauté the onion over medium heat. Stir in the sherry and cook for 1 minute over high heat, or until the liquid evaporates. Scrape this mixture into the pot with the water and bouquet garni. Drain the pears and add to the soup pot with the turnips. Add the salt, bring to a boil, lower the heat and simmer for about 10 minutes, or until the vegetables are tender. Remove from the stove and discard the bouquet garni, squeezing to extract all the juices. Purée the soup in a blender or food processor.

Prepare the garnish by cooking the hominy in butter for 2 minutes, then adding the lemon juice. To serve, reheat in a double boiler and stir in the cream at the last minute. Fill heated bowls with the soup, and place a tablespoon of sautéed hominy and a sprig of mint in each bowl.

POTAGE AUX TROIS FROMAGES

You can serve this soup in individual onion-soup bowls. I prefer to use a shallow heat-proof dish, such as a porcelain soufflé dish or a baking dish. That way, there's plenty of room for the cheese, croutons and half-melted cheese to blend together in a crunchy, delectable crust.

2 large Idaho potatoes	*1 bay leaf*
3 slices French bread, each	*6 ounces grated Gruyère, at*
½ inch thick	*room temperature*
4 tablespoons olive oil	*Coarse salt*
3 tablespoons flour	*6 ounces Jarlsberg, cut in*
¼ teaspoon dry mustard	*½-inch cubes, refrigerated*
5 cups milk	*4 ounces grated Parmesan*

Pare and cube the potatoes. Boil the cubes in salted water until they are done. Drain and set aside. Remove the crusts of the bread, cut the centers into cubes and sauté them in 1 tablespoon of olive oil until they are golden. Drain, set aside and discard the oil.

In a large saucepan, heat the remaining 3 tablespoons of olive oil and stir in the flour, cooking it over moderate heat to form a very pale roux. Stir in the mustard, remove the pan from the heat and whisk in the milk. Return to the heat and bring the sauce to a boil, whisking constantly. Add the bay leaf, lower the heat and cook for 10 to 15 minutes. You will have a rather thin white sauce. Remove from the heat, discard the bay leaf and add the grated Gruyère, whisking it vigorously until the cheese melts into the sauce. The hard whisking cools the sauce and allows you to blend in the cheese without having it curdle. If that should happen, however, there is nothing to do but start over again. Add a minimum of salt now, remembering that two other cheeses will be added when the soup is served.

Transfer the soup to a double boiler and cover it with buttered waxed paper. Set aside until you are ready to finish it for serving.

When you are ready to serve, reheat the soup in the double boiler until it is very hot. You can serve it in two ways. If you have individual bowls of the kind used for onion soup, divide the potatoes, croutons and Jarlsberg cubes among the bowls. Ladle in equal amounts of hot cheese soup, sprinkle with Parmesan, and place the bowls under a preheated broiler until the Parmesan melts and turns brown and crusty.

Or you can combine all the ingredients in a serving dish with a lot of surface and once again broil until the Parmesan melts and browns. Then ladle out the servings into preheated plates at the table, trying to keep some of the crusty top intact for each serving.

NEW JERSEY CHEESE-TOMATO SOUP

In mid-summer I get perfect tomatoes from New Jersey—meaty, with a good color, size and bouquet. If you have large home-grown tomatoes, they are probably even better. This is the ultimate tomato soup, in which the tomato becomes its own bowl: you touch it with the soup spoon and it collapses into the broth. I like to bake it high in the oven in a ceramic casserole so that the cheese topping turns golden. It's even better when each tomato casing is set in an individual casserole or onion-soup bowl.

4–5 pounds large ripe tomatoes (at least 1 per person)
6 tablespoons olive oil
2 cloves garlic, minced
¼ cup finely chopped onion
¼ cup finely chopped celery
¼ cup finely chopped carrot
2 fresh or dried hot peppers, seeded and chopped
1 tablespoon plus 2 teaspoons minced fresh thyme, oregano, basil or parsley
1 bay leaf

2 tablespoons tomato paste
1 tablespoon coarse salt
1½ cups white wine
8 ounces cream cheese
2 medium onions, peeled and cut in eighths
3 to 4 sprigs fresh thyme or other herb
4 ounces Parmesan cheese, cut in ¼-inch cubes
2 ounces Parmesan cheese, grated
3 ounces mozzarella, grated

Cut a cap ¾ inch deep from the top of each tomato. Remove the pulp with a teaspoon, leaving a sturdy casing. Combine caps and pulp and set aside.

In a saucepan, heat 4 tablespoons of oil and sauté the garlic, chopped onion, celery, carrot, peppers, 2 teaspoons of the herbs and the bay leaf for about 5 minutes. Add the tomato paste with the pulp and caps, the salt and 1 cup of the wine. Bring to a boil, reduce heat and simmer for 20 minutes. Remove the bay leaf and pass the soup through a food mill. Ladle 1 cup of the still-warm soup into a bowl with the cream cheese. Break up the cheese and return it and the soup to the saucepan.

Preheat the oven to 475°. Oil the bottom and sides of a 14-inch circular baking dish or an 8- by 12-inch rectangular dish. Put the tomato cases into the dish: they should fit tightly. Rub the onion pieces with oil and arrange them, with the sprigs of fresh thyme, around the tomatoes.

Place cubes of Parmesan in each tomato and pour the soup over them, filling each tomato to the brim and pouring the rest of the soup into the baking dish with the remaining ½ cup wine. Combine the grated Parmesan and mozzarella and sprinkle them over the tomatoes with the remaining tablespoon of chopped herbs. Set the dish high in the oven for 30 to 40 minutes, or until the cheese topping is golden brown and crusty.

To serve, bring the baking dish to the table. Very carefully, spoon one tomato into each preheated soup plate and then ladle on some of the broth.

To serve in individual ovenproof bowls, just put one tomato in each bowl, then proceed as above, adding some onion, fresh herbs and grated cheese to each bowl before you bake the soup.

Twenty New Beautiful Soups

ENRICHED STOCK

VEGETABLE SOUPS

Beet Soup
Chayote Soup
Chick-Pea Soup
Fava Bean and Vegetable Soup
Leek Soup
Onion Soup
Peanut Soup
Sweet Bell Pepper Soup
Sweet Potato Soup
Cream of Salsify Soup
Cold Sorrel Soup
Cream of Swiss Chard Soup
Watercress Soup

FISH SOUPS

Crabmeat and Cauliflower Soup
Oyster Chowder
Scallop and Shrimp Soup

MEAT SOUP

Lamb Broth

FRUIT SOUPS

Peach Soup
Cream of Persimmon Soup
Strawberry Soup

ENRICHED STOCK

There are many ways to enrich a stock. This enriched amber-colored stock is excellent served with an array of julienned vegetables and/or fresh herbs. It also makes a magnificent base for the preparation of all kinds of soups.

2 teaspoons olive or vegetable
  oil
2 cloves garlic, crushed
1 jalapeño pepper, seeded and
  chopped, 1 or 2 dried red hot
  chili peppers, or a pinch of
  cayenne
1½-inch piece fresh ginger,
  chopped
1 medium leek, washed and
  chopped
1 medium yellow or red onion,
  chopped
3 celery tops, washed and
  chopped

1 small carrot, washed and
  chopped
1 bay leaf
½ teaspoon fennel seeds
1 1-ounce bunch fresh thyme
  (¼ teaspoon dried) or
  2–3 sprigs fresh oregano
  (¼ teaspoon dried)
12–15 sprigs fresh dill or
  Italian parsley
7 cups Beef Stock (page 74),
  Chicken Stock (page 105),
  Vegetable Stock (page 3) or
  water

In a small stockpot, heat the oil. Stir in the garlic, hot pepper and ginger. Add the leek, onion, celery, carrot, bay leaf and fennel seeds and sauté, stirring now and then, over medium heat until the onion starts to turn golden around the edges. Add the fresh or dried thyme or oregano, dill, and the stock or water. Bring to a boil over high heat. Lower the heat, cover and simmer for 20 to 25 minutes. Remove from the heat and let cool slightly. Pour the enriched stock through a fine sieve or a strainer lined with a double layer of cheesecloth, pressing the vegetables and herbs against the sides of the strainer to extract all their juices, and discard them.

BEET SOUP

A healthy red beet, large or small, should be firm to the touch, with dark, smooth and unblemished skin. The flesh should be of the darkest red with a minimum or no trace of "whitish rings" or "veins." I like to use the stems and skins to enrich the stock or water base of the soup. An important seasoning of this soup is a good-quality wine vinegar, which enhances the sweetness of the beets.

To garnish, chop a few of the young pale-green leaves from the beets and sprinkle them on top of the soup along with dill, parsley or any other herb.

3 large beets
6½ cups Beef Stock (page 74),
  Chicken Stock (page 105),
  Vegetable Stock (page 3),
  Enriched Stock (page 159)
  or water
1 tablespoon olive or vegetable
  oil
1 small red or yellow onion,
  cut into ¼-inch dice, or
  whole peeled pearl onions
1 teaspoon sugar
2 tablespoons red wine vinegar
1 small carrot, peeled and cut
  into ¼-inch dice

1 medium potato, peeled and
  cut into ¼-inch dice
3 stalks celery, washed,
  deveined and cut into
  ¼-inch dice
⅓ cup fresh or frozen peas
Coarse salt

Garnish:
  3 tablespoons chopped fresh
    dill, coriander or basil
    leaves
  1 teaspoon sour cream for
    each serving (optional)
  6–8 sprigs purple basil
    (optional)

Under cold running water, thoroughly wash and scrape the beets. Peel the beets, reserving the skins and stems. Cut 2 of the peeled beets into ¼-inch dice and set aside. Julienne the remaining beet and set aside separately.

Heat the stock or water and add the reserved skins and stems. Cook for 5 to 10 minutes to enrich the stock, then remove and discard the skins and stems.

Meanwhile, in a straight-sided saucepan, heat the tablespoon of oil. Add the onion and sugar and sauté, stirring, until the onion is translucent. Add the vinegar and continue to cook, stirring, until all of the vinegar has evaporated. Add the carrot, potato, celery and reserved diced beets. Add the enriched stock or water and bring to a boil over high heat. Lower the heat, cover and gently simmer for 15 to 20 minutes, or until the vegetables are barely tender. Add the reserved julienned beet and cook for 3 minutes longer. Add the peas and continue to cook for about 2 more minutes. Correct the seasoning with salt to taste.

Sprinkle with the chopped dill, coriander or basil leaves and dot each serving with a teaspoon of the optional sour cream. Garnish the side of each soup plate with the optional sprigs of purple basil.

CHAYOTE SOUP

Chayote is a crisp and gently flavored pear-shaped summer squash with a taste reminiscent of a winter melon or a cross between a cucumber and a zucchini. Some varieties of chayotes have smooth skins and others have a hairbrushlike array of nonsticking prickles. The colors range from ice to apple-green to yellowish-creamy. Chayotes vary in size from large, weighing up to a pound, to medium, weighing about half a pound. You can sometimes find tiny underdeveloped chayotes weighing only a few ounces that are excellent when simply steamed and served as a vegetable. The best chayotes for this soup are medium or large vegetables in tip-top condition, firm, heavy and unblemished.

8 chayotes
4 cups Chicken Stock
(page 105), Vegetable Stock
(page 3) or water
1 tablespoon coarse salt
2 tablespoons olive oil
1 large clove garlic, peeled and
finely chopped
1–2 jalapeño peppers, seeded
and finely chopped

5 stalks celery, washed,
deveined and minced
(1 cup)
1 large onion, peeled and finely
chopped (about 2 cups)
1 teaspoon ground fennel
¼ teaspoon ground allspice

Garnish:
2 tablespoons chopped fresh
dill

Peel the chayotes and cut them into quarters lengthwise. Remove the large seeds with a sharp paring knife and discard them. Cut an equivalent of 2 of the largest chayotes into about ¼-inch cubes. Chop the remaining chayotes. Set aside. In a saucepan, bring the stock or water and salt to a boil. Add the 2 cubed chayotes and blanch them for about 3 minutes, or until barely tender. Remove with a slotted spoon and reserve. Measure the stock or water. You should have 4 cups; if not, add enough water to make 4 cups. Set aside.

In an enameled or stainless steel saucepan, heat the olive oil. Add the garlic, hot peppers and celery and sauté over medium-low heat for about 2 to 3 minutes. Add the onion, fennel and allspice and continue to cook for about 5 more minutes, or until the onion is translucent. Do not brown. Stir in the remaining chopped chayotes. Add the 4 cups of reserved stock or water and bring to a boil. Lower the heat and simmer, uncovered, for 20 minutes. Remove from the heat and blend in several batches in a blender or food processor at top speed until totally smooth. Return the blended soup to the saucepan and stir in the blanched chayotes. Heat thoroughly, stirring constantly, over a very low flame, or reheat and keep hot in a double boiler until ready to serve.

Correct the seasoning with more salt to taste and serve hot, garnished with the chopped dill.

CHICK-PEA SOUP

Chick-peas have an earthy flavor (somewhat resembling the taste of roasted nuts) and a mealy quality that produces richly textured and delicious soups. To prepare this legume and the whole family of dried beans and peas, thoroughly rinse them in cold water first to remove any dirt and then tenderize them by soaking them in water overnight. Use the strained soaking liquid as the base for the soup. Other beans, such as white beans, canary beans, flageolets or lima beans, will produce an equally satisfying and exciting soup.

One of the charms of this soup is its magnificent texture. For an even smoother texture, force all the soup, before blending, through a mouli or food mill, leaving only the tough skins behind. Then proceed with the blending and finish the soup.

1 pound dried chick-peas (about 2¼ cups) or 3 19-ounce cans chick-peas (see note, page 164)
10 cups cold water
1 bay leaf
2 tablespoons olive oil
2 cloves garlic, peeled and finely chopped
1-inch piece fresh ginger, peeled and finely chopped
1 jalapeño pepper, seeded and finely chopped
2 large leeks, white part only, washed and finely chopped (1 cup)
1 onion, peeled and finely chopped (about 1⅔ cups)

1 teaspoon ground cumin
⅛ teaspoon ground mace
1 pinch ground cinnamon
2 large stalks celery, washed, deveined and finely chopped (1 cup)
1 tablespoon coarse salt
2 small bunches fresh spinach, washed, leaves removed and thinly sliced (2 cups loosely packed)

Garnish:
⅛ pound boiled ham, thinly sliced and julienned
¼ pound fresh lump crabmeat or cooked tiny shrimp

Place the dried chick-peas in a strainer or colander and wash them thoroughly under cold running water. Soak the washed chick-peas overnight in the cold water. Drain them thoroughly, reserving the soaking liquid. Measure out 2 cups of the chick-peas and set aside the remaining 4 cups. Place the soaking liquid, the 2 cups of chick-peas and the bay leaf in a saucepan and cook over medium heat for 45 minutes, or until tender. Drain chick-peas and set aside, discarding the bay leaf. Measure the cooking liquid and add enough water if necessary to make 8 cups. Set aside.

In a saucepan, heat the olive oil. Add the garlic, ginger, hot pepper and leeks and sauté over medium heat until the leeks have wilted, about 4 minutes. Add the onion, cumin, mace and cinnamon and cook, stirring, until the onion is translucent, about 5 minutes. Do not brown the onion. Stir in the celery, then add the remaining 4 cups of reserved chick-peas.

Add the 8 cups of reserved cooking liquid and bring to a boil over high heat. Lower the heat, cover and simmer, stirring from time to time, for 45 minutes, or until the chick-peas are very tender. Add the salt and stir. Remove from the heat and blend in several batches in a blender or food processor. Place the soup in an enameled saucepan and add the 2 cups of reserved cooked chick-peas. Heat thoroughly, stirring constantly, over very low heat, or reheat in a double boiler and keep hot until ready to serve. Correct the seasoning with more salt to taste. Just before serving, quickly mix in the thinly sliced spinach leaves and garnish the center of each serving with the julienned ham and lumps of crabmeat or shrimp.

NOTE: If the soup thickens too much, add just enough milk, chicken stock or water while blending to obtain a slightly looser consistency.

If using canned chick-peas, rinse them under cold running water and drain; you should have 6 cups. Omit the first step in the recipe. Use 4 cups of the chick-peas and 5 cups of water or chicken stock instead of the 8 cups called for above; after the chick-peas have been added, cook them for only 20 minutes. Fold in the remaining 2 cups of chick-peas at the end of the cooking.

FAVA BEAN AND VEGETABLE SOUP

Fresh fava beans cook very quickly and have a wonderful flavor. Dry ones are equally good. Soak them overnight with enough cold water to cover, drain and use as you would the fresh beans.

*5 pounds fresh fava beans
(1¼ pounds already shelled
and skinned) or 8 ounces dry
fava beans
3 stalks celery, washed, tops
trimmed and saved and
stalks cut into ¼-inch slices
6 large cloves garlic, crushed
with skin
12–18 black peppercorns
2–3 sprigs fresh coriander,
oregano or Italian parsley
1 bay leaf
8 whole cloves*

*8 cups water, Chicken Stock
(page 105) or Beef Stock
(page 74)
2 tablespoons coarse salt
1 onion, peeled and cut into
¼-inch cubes
1 carrot, peeled and cut into
¼-inch cubes
1 potato, peeled and cut into
¼-inch cubes*

*Garnish:
2 tablespoons chopped fresh
coriander or Italian
parsley*

If using fresh fava beans, shell them in the following manner: pop open each pod by pressing the seam near the stem end, then run your thumbnail down the seam to split it. Expose the beans and remove them. With the tip of a paring knife or your thumbnail, split the protective skin lengthwise on each bean in order to pull away the skin in one piece, or make a slit on the curved side of the beans and remove the tough, rubbery outer skin, being careful not to bruise the delicate beans. Set aside.

In a stockpot, place the celery tops, crushed garlic, peppercorns, coriander, oregano or Italian parsley, bay leaf, cloves, water or stock and salt and bring to a boil. Lower the heat, cover the stockpot and simmer for 30 minutes. Remove from the heat and strain through a fine sieve or chinoise. Measure the broth. You should have 6 cups. If not, add enough water or extra stock to make 6 cups.

In a soup kettle or saucepan, add the broth, onion, carrot, sliced celery and potato and bring to a boil. Lower the heat and let simmer for 8 minutes. Add the fava beans and continue to simmer for another 5 minutes, or until the beans are barely cooked. Remove from the heat.

Correct the seasoning with more salt to taste. Serve hot, garnished with the chopped coriander or Italian parsley.

VARIATION: To use meat in this recipe select about 3 pounds of a flavorful beef cut, such as chuck or shank. Section the meat into 6 to 8 handsome servings, calculating 1 piece per person. Place the meat in the stockpot along with the celery tops, garlic, herbs, spices and 10 cups of water or stock. Add the salt and bring to a boil. Lower the heat, cover and gently simmer, stirring now and then, for about 2 hours, or until the meat is tender. Remove the chunks of meat from the stock and set aside. Strain through a fine sieve or chinoise and let the stock sit undisturbed until the fat has risen to the surface, about 5 minutes. Remove and discard all the fat. Measure the stock and add enough water if necessary to make 6 cups. Return the meat to the cleaned broth and proceed with the recipe, adding the vegetables in the appropriate order.

LEEK SOUP

Select leeks that have not been trimmed, as they will keep longer and most likely will be fresher. Smaller leeks with long white bases are usually best. Avoid leeks that look wilted and have yellowish leaves or woody centers.

For this soup use only the white part to achieve an attractive light-colored soup. Save the green leaves for the stockpot. Leeks need to be cleaned well because they are very sandy. First trim off the green part, then trim off the roots and cut the shaft in half lengthwise. Soak the vegetables in cold water to soften the dirt, and rinse them thoroughly under running water. Drain.

6–8 medium leeks, white part
only
2 tablespoons vegetable or olive
oil
2 large cloves garlic, peeled and
finely chopped
3 stalks celery, deveined and
finely chopped (1 cup)
2 large onions, peeled and
finely chopped (about
3 cups)
1 teaspoon ground fennel or
coriander seeds
1/4 teaspoon ground mace
Pinch of cayenne pepper
1 fully packed tablespoon
chopped fresh oregano, dill
or thyme leaves (from about
5 sprigs)

1 small potato, peeled and
finely chopped (1/3 cup)
5 cups water or Chicken Stock
(page 105)
1 tablespoon coarse salt

Garnish:
1 full tablespoon thinly
sliced chives
White part of 2 leeks, finely
sliced and very briefly
sautéed in 2 teaspoons
olive oil

Wash the leeks as described above and drain. Chop them to yield about 7 cups and set aside.

In a straight-sided saucepan, heat the oil. Add the garlic and celery and sauté over medium heat until the celery has softened, about 1 minute. Do not brown. Add the onions, ground fennel or coriander seeds, mace, cayenne pepper and cook, stirring, until the onions are translucent, about 4 to 5 minutes. Add the chopped leeks and oregano, dill or thyme and cook over low heat, stirring constantly, until the leeks have wilted, about 15 minutes. Add the chopped potato and water or chicken stock and salt. Bring to a boil over high heat. Lower the heat, cover and simmer, stirring from time to time, for 15 minutes.

Remove from the heat and purée the mixture in several batches at top speed in a blender or food processor. Reheat the soup in a double boiler and keep hot until ready to serve. Correct the seasoning with more coarse salt to taste. Serve the soup garnished with the sliced chives or leeks.

NOTES: If the soup appears too thick after it has been puréed, just add a little more water or chicken stock.

This soup can also be served cold. After blending, chill the soup thoroughly over ice or chill in the refrigerator for several hours. Correct seasoning with more coarse salt to taste.

For extra richness, whether the soup is served hot or cold, mix in about 2 to 3 tablespoons of crème fraîche.

ONION SOUP

When making onion soup, select a mild and sweet onion, such as one of the yellow varieties. They should feel firm, heavy and unblemished and their papery, silky skin should be dry and smooth; avoid soft or sprouting onions. A good beef stock is necessary to create a background and complement the great flavor of onions. Even better is an enriched beef stock (see page 159).

There are several ways to give the finished soup its final touch. Chopped fresh herbs and/or croutons are always good, as are freshly grated Parmesan and/or Gruyère. For an exciting and aromatic topping, ladle the hot soup into individual heat-resistant and warmed soup bowls, preferably ceramic, and cover most of the surface with a thin slice of white bread. Sprinkle with generous amounts of freshly grated cheese and immediately place the bowls under a hot broiler—as close to the source of heat as possible—just long enough for the cheese to melt and obtain an appetizing golden crust.

4 large yellow onions
3 tablespoons olive oil
1 large clove garlic, peeled and
    minced
¼ cup sweet vermouth
2 tablespoons soy sauce
    (preferably dark)

6 cups Beef Stock (page 74),
    Chicken Stock (page 105)
    or water
Coarse salt

Garnish:
    2 tablespoons chopped fresh
        dill or Italian parsley
    Croutons

Peel the onions. Cut them in half lengthwise and trim off the tops and bottoms. Thinly slice the onions lengthwise. You should have about 10 cups. Set aside.

In a large straight-sided saucepan, heat the olive oil. Stir in the garlic, but do not brown. Add the onions and sauté over high heat, stirring now and then, until the onions start to turn golden around the edges, about 35 minutes. Add the vermouth and soy sauce. Stir and cook until all the liquid has evaporated. Add the stock or water, bring to a boil and stir. Lower the heat and let simmer for 10 minutes. Correct the seasoning with salt to taste and remove from the heat. Serve garnished with the chopped fresh dill or parsley and/or croutons.

PEANUT SOUP

Early Peruvians cultivated, roasted and ate peanuts long before the arrival of the Spanish and Portuguese. Peanuts particularly complement and give distinctive flavor to other foods. Their crunchy texture and their ability to thicken soups, sauces and a variety of other dishes earn them a prominent place in any kitchen.

One of the interesting ways to enjoy all these great qualities in one dish is to put peanuts into the soup pot. To make a good peanut soup is as easy as sautéing some garlic, chopped onion and chopped leek in oil or butter until the vegetables have softened. Then mix in a good quantity of unsalted roasted and chopped peanuts, add water or milk or a combination of both, or a good light chicken stock, and let it simmer for about 10 minutes. Blend it all together to obtain a rich, smooth soup. Correct the seasoning with salt and white pepper to taste before serving. The following recipe takes this soup one step further by adding a variety of vegetables and garnishing with chopped fresh herbs. For a more complex soup using pork, see the variation at the end of the recipe.

4 small tomatoes
6 cups Chicken Stock
(page 105)
2 medium onions, peeled and
  cut into quarters
1 leek, white part mostly,
  washed and cut in half
1 large parsnip or carrot, peeled
3 dry mirasol/guajillo, ancho
  or serrano peppers, seeded
1 cup light beer
3 stalks celery, washed,
  deveined and chopped
  (about 1 cup)

1 cup unsalted peanut butter
  (9 ounces)
1 tablespoon coarse salt
⅓ cup shelled roasted peanuts
2 medium potatoes, peeled and
  cut into 1¼-inch cubes

Garnish:
  1 ear corn on the cob,
    cooked and cut into 6–8
    equal slices
  2 tablespoons chopped fresh
    coriander or Italian
    parsley

Blanch the tomatoes for a few seconds in a pot of boiling water, then remove them from the water. When they are cool enough to handle, cut out the conical plugs and peel the tomatoes with the point of a paring knife. Cut the peeled tomatoes in half crosswise and squeeze the juice and seeds into a strainer set over a bowl. Discard the seeds. Mince the tomato pulp, add it to the juice and set aside.

Place the chicken stock, onions, and leeks in a saucepan and bring to a boil. Lower the heat and simmer for a few minutes. Add the parsnip or carrot and continue to cook for about 25 minutes, or until the parsnip or carrot is tender. Remove from the heat and strain, reserving the vegetables separately from the broth. Measure the broth and add extra stock or water if necessary to make 5 cups. Set aside.

Place the hot peppers and the beer in a small bowl and let soak for 20 minutes, or until soft.

Pour the soaked peppers and the beer into a blender or food processor and blend thoroughly. Add the tomatoes with their juice and celery and continue to blend. Then add the cooked vegetables together with 2 cups of the reserved chicken broth. Blend in several batches, if necessary, until smooth. The total yield should be 8 cups; if it is not, add more chicken stock or water.

Add the peanut butter, puréed pepper-vegetable mixture, remaining 3 cups of chicken broth and salt. Bring to a boil, stirring now and then. Lower the heat and simmer over a low flame for about 10 minutes. Add the peanuts and potatoes and continue to cook for 45 minutes, or until the potatoes are tender. Correct the seasoning with more salt to taste. Garnish the soup with the slices of corn and serve piping hot, sprinkled with fresh coriander or Italian parsley.

NOTE: If a thinner soup is desired, mix in an extra cup of chicken stock.

VARIATION: Wipe 3 pounds pork rump with a damp cloth and cut into 2-inch cubes. In a mortar and pestle pound 3 peeled garlic cloves, 1 tablespoon coarse salt, 2 teaspoons ground cumin seeds, 1 teaspoon chili powder, and ⅛ teaspoon ground cloves to a smooth paste. Add ¼ cup vinegar (red wine, sherry or cider) and mix well. Let sit for about 5 minutes. Blend in 2 tablespoons of achiote oil (see page 42) and rub this mixture into the cubed pork. Let the meat marinate, well covered, for 4 hours at room temperature or overnight in the refrigerator. Heat 2 tablespoons of achiote oil in a saucepan. Add the pork and the marinade and sear the meat on all sides over medium heat for about 8 to 10 minutes. At this point add the peanut butter and stir until all the meat pieces are well coated. Add the puréed pepper-vegetable mixture, remaining 3 cups of chicken broth and salt. Bring to a boil, stirring occasionally, then lower the heat. Simmer for 1 hour and 30 minutes over a very low flame, or until the meat is barely tender. Add the peanuts and potatoes and continue to cook until the potatoes are tender, about 45 minutes. Correct the seasoning with more salt to taste. Garnish the soup as above.

SWEET BELL PEPPER SOUP

Red and yellow peppers are the sweetest of the bell peppers, and roasting brings out their natural taste and sweetness. Cook peppers in a roasting pan in a 450°F. oven for about 40 minutes until the skin is loose. Or roast them under a broiler for about 25 minutes, turning frequently to brown evenly. When the peppers are cool enough to handle, peel off the skin and remove the seeds.

8 large red bell peppers, roasted
1 tablespoon coarse salt
2 teaspoons granulated white
sugar
1/8 teaspoon ground allspice
1/8 teaspoon ground cloves
1 teaspoon ground fennel or
cumin seeds
1 large pinch saffron, optional
1/2 cup semisweet sherry, dry
vermouth or Pernod
3 sprigs fresh coriander
3 sprigs fresh thyme
3–4 sprigs fresh mint
2 stalks celery, each about
4 inches long
5 large ripe tomatoes

3 tablespoons olive oil
1 jalapeño pepper, seeded and
finely chopped
1/2-inch piece fresh ginger,
peeled and finely chopped
1 onion, peeled and finely
chopped (about 2 cups)
2 leeks, white part only, washed
thoroughly and finely
chopped (about 1 1/4 cups)
1 small carrot, peeled and
grated (1/3 cup)
3 cups water

Garnish:
2 tablespoons chopped fresh
dill

Coarsely chop 5 of the roasted peppers and set aside. Thinly slice 2 peppers, about ⅛ inch thick, and set aside. Section the remaining pepper lengthwise into 6 to 8 equal strips and set aside.

In a cup or small bowl mix the salt, sugar, allspice, cloves, fennel or cumin seeds, saffron, if using, and sherry, vermouth or Pernod. Let this mixture sit for about 10 minutes to soften.

Make a bouquet garni by folding and placing the coriander, thyme and mint between the 2 concave sides of the celery stalks. Press the stalks tightly together to contain the herbs and tie the length of the entire bouquet securely with kitchen string.

Blanch the tomatoes for a few seconds in a pot of boiling water, then remove them from the water. When they are cool enough to handle, cut out the conical plugs and peel the tomatoes with the point of a paring knife. Cut the peeled tomatoes in half crosswise and squeeze the juice and seeds into a strainer set over a bowl. Discard the seeds and reserve the juice. Finely chop the tomato halves and set aside.

In a straight-sided saucepan, heat the oil. Add the hot pepper, ginger and onion and sauté until the onion is translucent, about 3 to 4 minutes. Add the leeks and grated carrot and continue sautéing for another 3 minutes. Add the softened spices and juice from the tomatoes (1 cup—if you don't have a full cup, add enough water to make 1 cup) and cook gently over low heat until most of the liquid has evaporated, about 10 minutes. Add the chopped tomatoes and cook, stirring, until all the liquid has evaporated, about 10 to 15 minutes. Add the chopped peppers and continue to cook for about 5 minutes, stirring continuously. Add the bouquet garni and water. Bring to a boil, lower the heat and cover. Let simmer for 20 to 25 minutes, stirring now and then.

Remove from the heat and blend in several batches in a blender or food processor until smooth. Fold in the reserved thinly sliced peppers and decorate the top of the soup with the strips of pepper. Serve garnished with the chopped dill.

SWEET POTATO SOUP

The difference between yams and sweet potatoes is so subtle that the two are often confused with one another, and with good reason—they can be and are used interchangeably. Yams are slightly more elongated with pinkish light-orange skins and a softer texture, but both are ideal for the soup pot.

Sweet potatoes or yams are best when they are small to medium in size. They should be firm, unblemished, smooth and not too misshapen. Avoid dull, dry, or shriveled ones and any with bruises, for rot spreads quickly.

I grew up loving sweet potatoes, and to this day I cannot help cooking more than I need, especially when I have baked them. If you have some leftover cooked or baked sweet potatoes or yams, simply peel them and use them in place of the raw ones in this recipe.

3 tablespoons olive oil
2 large leeks, white part only,
*   washed, drained and finely*
*   chopped (about 1 cup)*
2 large onions, peeled and
*   finely chopped (about*
*   3 cups)*
1 teaspoon sugar
⅛ teaspoon ground mace
½ teaspoon ground turmeric
2 small sweet potatoes or yams,
*   peeled and chopped (about*
*   4 cups)*
6 cups water, Chicken Stock
*   (page 105), milk or a*
*   mixture of ½ milk and ½*
*   water or light stock*

1 bouquet garni:
*   5 celery tops*
*   6 sprigs fresh Italian*
*   parsley*
*   6 sprigs fresh mint*
*   12 juniper berries, crushed*
*   wrapped and tied in a piece*
*   of cheesecloth, measuring*
*   about 10 by 10 inches*
1 tablespoon coarse salt
White pepper

Garnish:
*   1 small baked sweet potato*
*   2 tablespoons chopped fresh*
*   mint*

In a straight-sided saucepan, heat the olive oil. Add the leeks and sauté, stirring, for a few minutes until the leeks have wilted. Add the onions, sugar, mace and turmeric and mix well. Add the chopped sweet potatoes, water, stock or milk and the bouquet garni. Bring to a boil, skimming as the scum rises to the surface. Lower the heat and simmer, uncovered, until the sweet potatoes are cooked and very tender, about 30 minutes.

If you are using already cooked sweet potatoes, you need simmer the soup for only 5 minutes to heat the potatoes. Remove from the heat and discard the bouquet garni. Blend in several batches in a blender or food processor at high speed until very smooth. Add the salt and white pepper to taste. Reheat in an enameled saucepan over very low heat, stirring, or heat and keep hot in a double boiler until ready to serve. Cut the baked sweet potato in half and scoop out about 1 teaspoon of the flesh, placing it in the center of each serving. Garnish with the chopped mint and serve hot.

CREAM OF SALSIFY SOUP

Salsify, a very gently flavored vegetable root, commonly known as oyster plant, makes a terrific soup. There are two types of salsify, white and black; both are used interchangeably in the kitchen, the black one being fleshier and less fibrous. The roots should be firm and medium in size. If you can find salsify with its young narrow grassy leaves, use the leaves in a salad or lightly sauté them in sweet butter or a good olive oil, then season with a few grains of coarse salt, black pepper and a few drops of vinegar or lemon juice. The tender young leaves make a swell garnish for this soup.

2 pounds black or white salsify
  (about 10 roots)
3 tablespoons olive oil
1 large clove garlic, peeled and
  chopped
1 large onion, peeled and
  chopped (about 2 cups)
2 leeks, white part only, washed
  and chopped (1 cup)
¼ teaspoon ground mace
⅛ teaspoon (a pinch) cayenne
  pepper
3 stalks celery, washed,
  deveined and chopped
  (1 cup)

5-ounce piece baking potato,
  peeled and chopped (about
  ⅔ cup)
5 cups Chicken Stock (page
  105) or Vegetable Stock
  (page 3)
1 tablespoon coarse salt

Garnish:
  3 tablespoons chopped fresh
  dill

Scrub, trim and peel the salsify. Rinse them clean, chop them, and set them aside. To avoid discoloration, submerge the peeled salsify in cold water to which a few drops of lemon juice or vinegar have been added. When ready to use, drain thoroughly and proceed with the recipe.

In an enameled saucepan, heat the olive oil. Add the garlic, onion, leeks, mace, cayenne pepper and sauté, stirring, until the onion is translucent, about 4 minutes. Do not brown. Add the celery and continue to cook over medium heat until the celery has wilted. Add the chopped salsify, stir and cook for 1 minute longer. Add the potato, chicken or vegetable stock and salt. Bring to a boil, lower the heat and simmer, stirring now and then, for 10 minutes, or until the potato and the salsify are very tender. Remove from the heat and blend in several batches at top speed in a blender or food processor until smooth. If the soup thickens too much, add a little extra stock or milk.

Place the blended soup in an enameled saucepan and heat thoroughly, stirring, over a very low flame, or reheat and keep hot in a double boiler until ready to serve. Correct the seasoning with more salt to taste. Serve garnished with the chopped dill.

COLD SORREL SOUP

I have always had a passionate love affair with sorrel, a lemony-tasting perennial sour herb also known as Round or French Sorrel, Sour Grass and, in different varieties, Dock, Sour Dock, Dock Sorrel, Bitter Dock and Sheep Sorrel. We can use this great herb to create a splendid herbal soup. It can be served chilled or hot.

Select sorrel with small young leaves that are less pungent than the larger ones and avoid wilted and yellow leaves. If necessary, the herb can be wrapped in moist towels and kept fresh for a few days in the refrigerator, but it is best to use it as soon as it is obtained.

1–1¼ pounds sorrel
2 tablespoons olive oil
1-inch piece fresh ginger, peeled
*   and chopped*
1 jalapeño pepper, seeded and
*   chopped*
1 large onion, peeled and
*   chopped (about 2 cups)*
⅛ teaspoon ground cloves
½ teaspoon sugar
¼ cup Pernod

3 stalks celery, washed,
*   deveined and chopped*
*   (about 1 cup)*
2 cucumbers, peeled, seeded
*   and chopped*
2 small green bell peppers,
*   seeded and chopped (2 cups)*
1 tablespoon coarse salt
2½ cups water
White pepper

Wash the sorrel and drain well. Remove all the stems and chop them. Set aside. Separate 10 to 12 of the freshest and greenest leaves and set aside. Chop the remaining sorrel leaves and set aside.

In an enameled saucepan, heat the olive oil. Add the ginger, hot pepper, onion and cloves and sauté until the onion is translucent. Do not brown the onion. Add the sugar and Pernod and continue to cook, stirring, until all the liquor has evaporated. Add the celery, cucumbers, green peppers and chopped sorrel stems and cook, stirring, for a few minutes longer. Add the salt and water and bring to a boil. Lower the heat and simmer briefly for about 3 to 5 minutes.

Remove from the heat, let cool slightly (about 1 to 2 minutes) and stir in the chopped sorrel. Let sit undisturbed for another 3 to 4 minutes. Blend in several batches at top speed in a blender or food processor until smooth and strain through a fine sieve. Place the blended and strained soup in a large bowl and chill for several hours in the refrigerator. Correct the seasoning with more salt and white pepper to taste. Cut the reserved sorrel leaves into thin strips and serve the cold soup garnished with the shredded leaves.

NOTES: If you want a richer consistency, blend in 2 tablespoons of crème fraîche or heavy cream and garnish as above.

To present and serve this soup hot, serve it immediately after it has been blended. Or reheat in an enameled saucepan over a low flame; correct the seasoning with more salt to taste and garnish with shredded fresh sorrel leaves. For additional texture, add chunks of diced cooked potatoes or yuca or peeled, seeded and cubed or diced blanched chayotes while reheating the soup.

CREAM OF SWISS CHARD SOUP

Swiss chard, with its large green leaves and thin white or fleshy pale flat stalks, is somewhat similar to spinach. Swiss chard has two distinctive parts: sweet leaves, which have a slightly bitter yet attractive undertone, and the juicy stalks with their earthy aromatic flavor. By using both the leaves and the stalks together yet cooking them differently to promote contrast in texture and variety of taste, we can create this magnificent soup.

2 pounds Swiss chard

2 tablespoons olive oil

2 large cloves garlic, peeled and
finely chopped

1 or 2 jalapeño, arbol or
Anaheim peppers, seeded
and finely chopped

4 stalks celery, washed,
deveined, and finely
chopped (2 cups)

⅛ teaspoon ground cloves

⅛ teaspoon ground nutmeg

1 teaspoon ground cumin

1 large onion, peeled and finely
chopped (2 cups)

1 teaspoon coarse salt

1 cup (8 ounces) canned chick-
peas, rinsed and drained

5 cups Chicken Stock
(page 105) or water

3 tablespoons crème fraîche or
heavy cream

Wash the Swiss chard well and drain thoroughly. Remove 6 to 8 of the widest and freshest stems and thinly julienne. Place them in a bowl containing ice water and set aside. Chop the rest of the Swiss chard (leaves and stems) and set aside.

In a saucepan, heat the oil. Add the garlic, hot peppers, celery, cloves, nutmeg and cumin. Cook, stirring, over medium heat until the celery is soft, about 3 to 5 minutes. Add the onion and salt and continue to cook, stirring now and then, for 5 minutes longer, or until the onion is totally translucent. Add the chick-peas and chopped Swiss chard and cook, stirring now and then, until the Swiss chard has wilted, about 8 to 10 minutes. Add the stock or water and bring to a boil. Lower the heat and simmer gently for 10 minutes. Remove from the heat, place in a blender or food processor and blend in several batches until smooth.

Pour the soup into a double boiler and add the crème fraîche. Mix thoroughly. Correct the seasoning with more salt to taste. Drain the julienned Swiss chard stems well. Serve the soup piping hot, garnished with the julienned stems.

WATERCRESS SOUP

Watercress, a plant with delicate vivid green leaves, juicy stems and an attractive herbal peppery taste, is usually served raw, with a few drops of fine olive oil, lemon juice, salt and pepper in salads, or as an herb or garnish. When watercress is treated as a vegetable, it can be prepared in the form of a magnificent soup. Look for fresh, deep-green, crisp leaves and tender stems (thick stems give too strong a peppery flavor). Watercress is perishable, and if not used immediately, should be stored in the refrigerator wrapped in moist towels or with the stems in water and the leaves wrapped in damp towels.

Cook very briefly for a minute or so, just long enough to mellow the peppery taste somewhat.

*3 bunches watercress, rinsed
    clean and well drained*
2 tablespoons olive oil
*½-inch piece ginger, peeled and
    finely minced*
*1 large onion, peeled and finely
    chopped (about 2 cups)*
*4 stalks celery, washed,
    deveined and finely chopped
    (about 1½ cups)*
*1 teaspoon ground coriander
    seeds*

¼ teaspoon ground mace
*1 tablespoon fresh lime or
    lemon juice*
½ cup dry vermouth
*1 medium potato, peeled and
    finely chopped (about
    1¼ cups)*
*5½ cups Chicken Stock
    (page 105) or water*
*½ cup milk, heavy cream or
    half-and-half*
Coarse salt

Reserve 1 or 2 of the freshest sprigs of watercress per serving and place in cold water. Set aside.

Cut off and discard all the thick stems from the watercress, leaving the leaves and thin young stems; coarsely chop them, making about 4 cups. Set aside.

In a saucepan, heat the oil. Add the ginger, onion, celery, coriander and mace. Sauté, stirring, over medium heat until the onion is totally translucent, about 3 to 4 minutes. Add the lemon juice and cook for a few seconds longer. Add the vermouth and continue to cook, stirring, until all liquid has evaporated. Add the potato and stock or water and bring to a boil. Lower the heat and simmer gently until the potato is done, about 8 to 10 minutes. Add the chopped watercress, stir and continue to cook for 1 minute longer.

Remove from the heat and blend the soup in several batches in a blender or food processor until smooth. Heat the soup in a double boiler, add the milk or cream, mix well and correct the seasoning with salt to taste. Drain and dry the reserved sprigs of watercress. Remove a few leaves and place over the surface of the soup. Garnish the edge of the soup plate or the saucers of the soup cups with the sprigs of watercress and serve hot.

NOTE: This soup is also quite exquisite when served cold. After blending the soup, chill thoroughly over ice or for several hours in the refrigerator. Just before serving, mix in the milk or cream and correct the seasoning with salt to taste. Serve garnished as above.

CRABMEAT AND CAULIFLOWER SOUP

The distinct subtle taste and rich creamy texture produced by the cauliflower make a superb background to display the delicate and exquisite qualities of seafood. Here I use crabmeat for its sweet taste, but the soup is equally good with oysters, scallops or squid, as described below.

1 small head cauliflower
2 tablespoons safflower oil
1 jalapeño pepper, seeded and minced
2 leeks, white part only, washed and finely chopped (1 cup)
1 small cucumber, peeled, seeded and finely chopped (about ⅔ cup)
5½ cups Vegetable Stock (page 3), Fish Stock I (see page 39) or water

1 tablespoon coarse salt
2 tablespoons olive oil
1 large clove garlic, peeled and minced
1 pound fresh lump crabmeat
White pepper

Garnish:
2 tablespoons chopped fresh Italian parsley, tarragon or mint

Cut away and discard the leaves from the cauliflower. Wash and section the vegetable into florets, saving the thick main stem. Chop the florets, yielding about 4 cups. Peel and chop the stem and set aside with the chopped florets.

In a straight-sided saucepan, heat the safflower oil. Add the hot pepper and leeks and sauté over low heat, stirring now and then, until the leeks have wilted, about 5 minutes. Add the cucumber and stir. Continue to cook until the vegetables are soft, about 10 to 15 minutes longer. Add the stock or water and salt and bring to a boil, stirring now and then. Add the chopped cauliflower and simmer, uncovered, over low heat for 20 minutes, skimming from time to time. When the cauliflower is tender, remove from the heat and blend in several batches in a blender or food processor until smooth. Reheat the blended soup in an enameled saucepan over very low heat, stirring, or reheat and keep hot in a double boiler until ready to serve.

In a skillet, heat the olive oil. Add the minced garlic and sauté for a few seconds over low heat. Add the crabmeat and cook, gently shaking the skillet and being careful not to break up the crabmeat lumps, over a high flame until the crabmeat has just warmed through, about 3 minutes. Remove from the heat and fold the warm crabmeat under the hot soup. Correct the seasoning with more salt and white pepper to taste. Serve at once, garnished with chopped fresh herbs.

VARIATION: Strain 1½ pints of freshly shucked oysters, using the oyster liquor as part of the stock or water. Cook the oysters the same way as the crabmeat. Or substitute 1½ pounds sea or bay scallops: Wash and drain the scallops and add them to the soup instead of the crabmeat. Or use 1½ pounds of cleaned squid: Slice the body and fins on the diagonal into strips about ⅛ inch thick. If the tentacles are small, leave them whole; otherwise, cut them lengthwise in half or smaller. Add the squid to the skillet instead of the crabmeat.

OYSTER CHOWDER

The gentle bouquet of the sea together with the sexy quality of the oyster's taste and texture truly blooms in this luxurious and rejuvenating soup. Oysters—whether small, average or large, or from the East or West

Coast—should always be very fresh, with firmly closed shells. The meat should be plump, pale to pearl white, moist and accompanied by a scent of the sea. If the oysters are obtained already shucked, the liquor, the culinary term for the oysters' liquid, should be opaque, somewhat translucent but not milky. Oysters should be cooked just long enough to make them firm or to heat them through thoroughly.

2 pints shucked oysters with
*   their liquor*
4 cups whole milk
2 bay leaves
1 tablespoon coarse salt
1 tablespoon achiote seeds or 1
*   teaspoon paprika (optional)*
1 large clove garlic, peeled and
*   crushed*
2 dried hot red peppers, seeded
12–15 whole allspice berries
3 cups water
½-inch piece fresh ginger, sliced
1 large potato, peeled and cut
*   in ¼-inch dice*
8-ounce piece yuca

1 tablespoon olive oil
2 medium onions, peeled and
*   finely chopped (about*
*   2 cups)*
1 large leek, white part only,
*   finely chopped (about 1 cup)*
2 young stalks celery, washed,
*   deveined and finely chopped*
2 tablespoons unsalted butter
Kernels cut from 2 ears fresh
*   corn or 1 cup frozen corn*
*   kernels*

Garnish:
*   2 tablespoons chopped fresh*
*   Italian parsley or dill*

Strain the oysters into a bowl. Set the oysters aside and measure the liquor. You should have about 1½ cups.

In a saucepan over low heat, bring the milk, bay leaves, salt, optional achiote seeds or paprika, garlic, hot peppers and allspice slowly to a boil. Lower the heat and let simmer for 25 minutes. Strain the flavored milk through a fine sieve. Discard the contents of the strainer and save the milk. This will yield about 3½ cups. Set aside.

Meanwhile, in a small saucepan, bring the water to a boil with the sliced ginger. Lower the heat and simmer for about 5 minutes. Add the diced potato and continue to cook until tender, about 8 to 10 minutes. With a slotted spoon remove the potato and set aside; remove and discard the ginger. When the potato liquid is cool, measure it and add enough water if necessary to make 2 cups.

Peel the yuca and cut into quarters lengthwise. Remove and discard the central fibrous cord with a sharp paring knife. Chop the yuca. Pour the potato liquid into a blender or food processor and add the chopped yuca. Blend thoroughly at top speed for a minute or so. Pour the blended yuca through a strainer lined with a double layer of cheesecloth (or a fine sieve without a cheesecloth), pressing to extract all the juices from the pulp. Discard the cheesecloth and the pulp and set the strained yuca liquid aside until ready to use.

In a saucepan, heat the olive oil. Add the chopped onion and leek and sauté until the onion is translucent and the leek has wilted, about 4 minutes. Add the saved oyster liquor and mix. Thoroughly stir the yuca liquid. Add this liquid to the saucepan and bring to a boil over medium-high heat, stirring constantly. Lower the heat and simmer, stirring, until the mixture thickens, about 4 minutes. Add the strained milk and bring to a simmer again, stirring and scraping the bottom of the saucepan, for about 3 minutes. Remove from the heat and blend until smooth in several batches in a blender or food processor. Pour the soup and cooked potato into a double boiler. Reheat and keep warm until ready to use.

Heat the butter in a straight-sided saucepan over medium heat. Add the corn kernels and cook, stirring, for 3 to 4 minutes. Push the corn to the sides of the skillet and place the oysters in the middle. Quickly toss them over high heat for about 1 minute. Add the reheated soup and stir. Correct the seasoning with more salt to taste. Remove from the heat and serve at once, garnished with the chopped Italian parsley or dill.

SCALLOP AND SHRIMP SOUP

Shrimp of all sizes are right for this soup, provided they are fresh. If you buy whole shrimp, you can use the heads and shells to make a magnificent stock. Rich and full of shrimp flavor, the stock is unbeatable when making this soup. Sweet-water prawns, crawfish and langoustine—whole or just tails—are excellent substitutions for the shrimp, as are squid, oysters, abalone and clams.

1½–2 pounds large shrimp in
   the shell
1 pound sea scallops
6-ounce piece yuca
5 cups shrimp stock (see
   page 186), Fish Stock I (see
   page 39), Chicken Stock
   (page 105) or water
5 large tomatoes
3 large cloves garlic
3 jalapeño peppers
4 tablespoons olive oil
1 large onion, peeled and finely
   chopped (about 2 cups)

1 tablespoon coarse salt
1 bouquet garni:
   1 bunch fresh thyme
    (1 ounce)
   1 bunch fresh oregano
    (1 ounce)
   1 bay leaf
wrapped and tied in a piece
of cheesecloth, measuring
about 8 by 8 inches

Garnish:
   2 tablespoons chopped fresh
   dill

Rinse the shrimp under cold running water. Peel and devein them and set aside. Clean and drain the scallops and set aside. Peel the yuca and cut into quarters lengthwise. Remove and discard the central fibrous cord. Chop the yuca. Place 1 cup of the stock or water in a blender or food processor and add the chopped yuca. Blend thoroughly at top speed for 1 minute or so. Pour the liquid through a strainer lined with 2 layers of cheesecloth (or a fine sieve without cheesecloth), squeezing the cheesecloth to extract all the juices from the pulp. Discard the pulp and set the yuca liquid aside until ready to use.

Blanch the tomatoes for a few seconds in a pot of boiling water, then remove them from the water. When they are cool enough to handle, peel them with the point of a paring knife. Cut the peeled tomatoes in half crosswise and squeeze the juice and seeds into a strainer set over a bowl. Discard the seeds. Mince the tomato pulp, add it to the juice, and set aside.

Peel and mince 2 of the large cloves of garlic and set aside. Seed and mince 2 of the hot peppers and set aside.

In a saucepan, heat 2 tablespoons of the olive oil. Add the minced garlic, minced hot pepper and onion and stir. Add the tomatoes and juice and sauté, stirring, for 6 to 8 minutes. Add the remaining 4 cups of stock or water and salt. Thoroughly mix the yuca liquid and add to the stock. Bring to a boil, stirring constantly. Add the bouquet garni, lower the heat and simmer, stirring now and then, for 15 minutes. Correct the seasoning with more salt to taste. Set aside and keep hot.

In a straight-sided saucepan, heat the remaining 2 tablespoons of olive oil.

Meanwhile, peel and finely chop the remaining garlic clove and hot pepper. Add to the saucepan and stir. Add the shrimp and quickly toss over high heat just to sear them. Push the shrimp aside and add the scallops and quickly sear them on all sides. Pour the hot soup into the pan containing the seared shrimp and scallops and heat thoroughly. Correct the seasoning with more salt to taste if necessary and serve at once, garnished with the chopped dill.

NOTE: To make shrimp stock, crush or coarsely chop shrimp heads and shells and place them in a saucepan along with a finely chopped onion, a leek, a few stalks celery with tops, a carrot, a slice of fresh ginger and a few sprigs of herbs, such as fresh dill, mint, coriander or Italian parsley. Cover with about 5 cups of cold water, bring to a boil, stir and simmer over low heat for about 10 to 15 minutes. Cool slightly and strain the stock through a fine sieve or through a strainer lined with a double layer of cheesecloth.

LAMB BROTH

This light and delicious broth with ground lamb is the Peruvian equivalent to chicken soup, the all-American cure-all. For a clear, clean broth with a great bouquet, see the variation at the end of the recipe.

1½–2 pounds lamb neck
3 cloves garlic, slightly crushed
2 stalks celery with tops, cut
*   into pieces*
1–2 jalapeño peppers, cut into
*   3 pieces each*
1 bay leaf

2 tablespoons coarse salt
8 cups cold water

Garnish:
*   2 tablespoons chopped fresh*
*   mint or other herbs or*
*   julienned vegetables*

Thoroughly remove all the fat and fell from the lamb. Cut the meat into small pieces and place in a food processor. Process until the meat almost resembles a paste. Transfer to a bowl and set aside.

Place the garlic, celery, hot peppers, bay leaf, salt and water in a small stockpot and bring to a boil. Lower the heat to the lowest possible flame and cover the pot. Simmer for about 30 to 35 minutes, then strain through a fine sieve or a strainer lined with cheesecloth. You should still have 8 cups of liquid. Pour the liquid into a clean pot and bring to a boil. Remove 1 cup of the boiling liquid and pour it over the meat while stirring with a wire whisk. Then add another cup of the boiling liquid and stir. Whisk this mixture into the remaining 6 cups of the boiling broth and cook for about 1 minute. Remove from the heat and serve garnished with the mint or other herbs or julienned vegetables.

VARIATION: Before straining the broth, add the ground lamb and let it cook for about 2 minutes, then strain to eliminate the meat and vegetables.

PEACH SOUP

Peach soup is the most luxurious of soups. The simplest way to prepare it is to cook the fruits until they are very tender in enough water or white wine to cover and season with a few sticks of cinnamon, cloves and a bit of sugar. Once the peaches are cooked, peel them and discard the pits and spices. Blend the peaches with a little bit or all of their cooking liquid. Chill thoroughly and serve garnished with a sliced and julienned fresh peach. For a soup with a more complex flavor, follow the recipe below; it may also be served cold.

5 pounds peaches (about 8–10 peaches)
½ fresh pineapple about 2 pounds, without green tops
4 cups white wine
4–6 cups water
½ cup sugar
1 cinnamon stick (about 3 inches long)

1-inch piece fresh ginger, pared and cut in half
3 whole cloves
3 tablespoons heavy cream
4 teaspoons unsalted butter
2 cups canned white hominy, drained
2 tablespoons freshly squeezed lemon juice

Set aside about ¾ pound of the peaches for garnish. Rinse the remainder in cold water and drain in a colander.

Cut the pineapple in half lengthwise and cut away the core. Cut away the skin, reserving both the core and skin. Slice the pineapple into thick pieces and set aside.

In a large stainless steel sauté pan or stock pot (large enough to hold the peaches and pineapple, including the skin and core, in one layer), combine the wine, 4 cups of the water, sugar, cinnamon stick, ginger, cloves and all the pineapple pieces, including the skin and core, and bring to a boil over high heat. Lower the heat and let the liquid simmer for 30 minutes, partially covered, before adding the unpeeled peaches. When the liquid returns to a boil, lower the heat and let the fruit simmer for 30 to 45 minutes, adding the remaining water only if necessary to barely cover the contents of the pot. When the peach skins begin to wrinkle and the peaches offer no resistance when pierced with a fork, remove the pot from the stove and let cool until the fruit is easy to handle.

Cut the peaches in half, remove the pits and place the peaches in a bowl. With a slotted spoon remove the pineapple pieces and place them in a separate bowl.

Return the poaching liquid to the stove (still containing the pineapple skin, core and spices) and bring to a boil. Reduce the heat and let simmer, checking occasionally, for 30 minutes or so, or until the liquid reduces by about half. Strain the liquid; there should be about 3 cups.

Meanwhile, using the fine-gauge blade, purée the peaches in a food mill set over a large bowl, scraping the bottom of the blade frequently. Then purée the pineapple. (If you do not have a food mill, peel and pit the cooked peaches and purée the peaches and the pineapple in a food processor or blender.) There should be about 2 quarts of the mixture, which will be quite thick.

Stir 2 cups of the reduced poaching liquid into the fruit purée and place it in a double boiler to reheat. This may take as much as 20 to 25 minutes. When piping hot, the soup should have the consistency of a thick vichyssoise. Stir in the cream and taste for sweetness. Correct the seasoning with more sugar to taste and let the soup remain in the double boiler to keep hot while you prepare the garnish. If a thinner soup is desired, add as much of the remaining poaching liquid as necessary.

To prepare the garnish, drop the reserved ¾ pound peaches in boiling water for a minute or so and remove them with tongs. When cool enough to handle, peel them and remove the pits. Cut the peaches into fairly large pieces and stir them into the soup.

In a small saucepan, heat the butter and stir in the drained hominy. Toss the hominy about in the pan until it heats through. Stir in the lemon juice and heat for a moment. Serve the soup at once, garnished with a couple of tablespoons of the hominy placed in the center of each serving.

CREAM OF PERSIMMON SOUP

This unctuous soup can easily be served either before or after the main part of lunch or dinner. When the persimmons are truly ripe, the soup is so naturally sweet it can easily be considered a dessert. It looks most attractive served in chilled glass bowls.

*12 large or 15 small ripe
    persimmons
½ cup water
3 tablespoons lemon juice
1 teaspoon dried mustard*

*1 tablespoon sugar
⅛ teaspoon coarse salt
2 cups (16 ounces) yogurt
Fresh mint leaves (optional)*

Reserve 2 large persimmons or 3 small ones for garnish. To prepare the remaining persimmons, remove the flowerlike green from the stem end and cut away any discolored or damaged skin underneath. Scoop out as much of the persimmon meat as possible with a spoon, then place the persimmon, skin side down, on your work surface and scrape off as much as possible of the remaining meat, being careful not to include any skin. This procedure is somewhat tedious, but definitely worth the effort. Place the persimmon meat in a blender and add the water, lemon juice, mustard, sugar and salt and blend until the persimmons are smoothly puréed. You may have to do this in several batches. (A food processor will not give the same smooth texture as a blender, but can be used if necessary.) The persimmon purée should measure about 6 cups.

Refrigerate the purée in a fairly large ceramic, glass or stainless steel bowl. Let chill, stirring occasionally, for at least 6 hours or more, at which time the mixture will have become firm in places.

While the mixture is chilling, prepare the reserved persimmons. Set them on the stem end, and using a serrated knife, cut off the skins. Begin at the top and continue all around the circumference, then cut off and discard the entire stem ends. The persimmons should still be intact. Cut them into large pieces, discarding the cores. Cover with plastic wrap and refrigerate. Just before serving, remove the chilled purée from the refrigerator and whisk in the yogurt, combining the two until the mixture becomes a smooth, slightly opaque mixture. Taste for seasoning: it may profit from a little sugar, a pinch more salt or a few drops of lemon juice.

Serve in chilled glass bowls placed on small serving plates, and garnish with several pieces of cut-up persimmon in the center of each serving. For a color contrast, place the optional mint leaves at the edges of the serving plates—not in the soup itself.

NOTE: This soup is rich enough to allow smaller servings than usual. Six ounces is more than adequate and will allow you to increase the servings to ten.

STRAWBERRY SOUP

The gentle flavor and perfumy bouquet of strawberries is emphasized in this unique soup that can be served hot or cold.

When strawberries are picked before they have had a chance to ripen, they will never develop that intense sweet strawberry taste good for eating raw, but they are fine for the soup pot. Still, it is best to use ripe or slightly overripe berries, with or without bruises. Do not remove the caps of fresh strawberries until just before using, as the caps seal in the taste and protect the berries from spoiling.

Strawberries are highly perishable and should be kept in a cold and humid place and used as soon as possible. Or store berries for soup in a tightly closed container in the freezer with the caps removed, until you have collected enough to make them into a soup. The strawberries can go right from the freezer into the soup pot.

Most strawberries are relatively clean and only require wiping with a damp cloth to remove any grains of sand. If they must be washed, they should be quickly rinsed under running water in a colander and then drained. Never let strawberries soak in water; they will die right in front of your eyes, losing their bouquet and their texture.

6 pounds fresh strawberries
3 2-inch cinnamon sticks
1 dried hot red chili pepper
2 thin slices fresh ginger, peeled
½ cup sugar
1 tablespoon Calvados,
*   Cointreau or Triple Sec*

2 tablespoons crème fraîche or
*   heavy cream*

Garnish:
*   Crème fraîche (optional)*
*   Fresh mint leaves*

Rinse the strawberries very briefly under cold running water and let them drain thoroughly. Hull all the berries and set aside 8 to 10 of the largest and ripest ones for garnish.

Place the remaining strawberries in an enameled or stainless steel pot and add the cinnamon, hot pepper, ginger and sugar. Cover the pot and bring to boil, stirring, over medium heat. Remove the cover, lower the heat and let cook, stirring from time to time, for about 35 to 40 minutes. Remove from the heat and take out and discard the cinnamon, hot pepper and ginger. Blend the fruit in several batches at top speed in a blender or food processor until smooth. Pour the blended soup back into the cleaned pot and mix in the Calvados, Cointreau or Triple Sec. Heat the soup over a very low flame, or reheat and keep hot in a double boiler until ready to serve.

Meanwhile, cut the reserved strawberries into quarters or eighths, depending on their size, and set aside.

Correct the seasoning of the hot soup with more sugar to taste and mix in the crème fraîche or heavy cream. Add the reserved strawberry wedges and serve garnished with the optional dot of crème fraîche and mint leaves.

NOTE: This soup can also be served cold. After the strawberries are blended, mix in the Calvados, Cointreau or Triple Sec and refrigerate, stirring from time to time, for several hours. Correct the seasoning with more sugar to taste. Stir in the crème fraîche or heavy cream, mix in the strawberry wedges and serve garnished as above.

Index